The Power of Mental Wealth Featuring Jené M. Patrick

The Power of Mental Wealth Featuring Jené M. Patrick

Success Begins From Within

Jené M. Patrick
Johnny Wimbrey
Heather Monahan
Les Brown

WIMBREY TRAINING SYSTEMS
SOUTHLAKE, TEXAS

Table of Contents

Foreword

The world has become a more unpredictable and threatening place over the last year. Our ability to survive and thrive has been tested by tremendous outside forces that aren't in our control. Among the few things we can control are our perceptions and our thoughts.

The Power of Mental Wealth is a book I'm very proud to publish, especially at this moment in human history. This is a time for us to invest in our minds and not squander our mental resources.

Mental *wealth* is a cutting edge-concept, one you may not have heard much about just yet. The concept of mental wealth is just beginning to gain traction as people start to realize its possibilities and immense value.

So how is it different from mental health? Or mental strength? Is it something you can bring to the bank?

More than twenty immensely talented people share their de nitions of this term and their mental gifts with you in *The Power of Mental Wealth*. Their chapters include stories of perseverance, overcoming adversities, building self-con dence, increasing their joy, and training themselves to see the brilliance and success of their futures.

In every single case, they worked hard to perfect themselves and improve their minds. They worked on this intensely, investing a good chunk of their time, for years. They all succeeded, and so can you.

Not one of these authors suggests their gifts were just handed to them. They built their mental wealth the old-fashioned way, and they're sharing their results with you. They share the tools they use, such as listening, using their subconscious or all their senses, and building self-worth. They've learned to believe in themselves, create their own realities, and live life by design.

They have mastered the power of their wills.

I am awed by their potential, and even more, awed by their generosity in sharing what they've learned with you.

You can build your mental wealth through what you learn in this book. As world-famous Les Brown writes in his chapter, *grow continuously.*

Invest in your mind. It's the best investment you can make.

—Johnny Wimbrey

Chapter 1

The Power of Your Will

Johnny Wimbrey

They say a mind is a terrible thing to waste. I'll take this further: I say it's terrible, even unforgivable if you don't commit yourself to strengthening your mental powers and turning them into your strongest assets.

And, honestly, I'm amazed every day by the potential we all have. We are the only beings with the power of self-will. This means that we all possess the mental capacity to obey or to disobey, to lie or to be honest, to love or to hate, and the mental strength to will ourselves past adverse situations to reach our goals. (Setting those goals is a whole other book; I'll tell you about Building a Millionaire Mindset later in this chapter.

None of us are immune to adversity, none are immune to temptation, and none are immune to life's trials and tribulations. Whether we'd like to admit it or not, we all fall short in life at one point or another. Every human being will experience the good, the bad, and the ugly. That's the reality of life. Some situations may seem very small and trivial to most people, but these trivial situations can and do escalate to very regrettable and drastic situations.

We all have faults.

They say confession is good for the soul, so let me come clean to you:

I have no tolerance for people who are late or situations that waste time. I can't stand to be late, and I hate being unproductive. I cherish time because it's irreplaceable; you can never get it back once it's gone. People who are not time-conscious frustrate me. Actually, they drive me crazy.

> **We can develop the mental wealth to be able to afford our dreams, and the mental strength to keep us on track.**

I wasn't born watching a clock; I programmed myself to be time-conscious a long time ago when I was very young. You may be thinking, What's wrong with this? Valuing time is a strength, an excellent tool for someone with ambition, especially for a leader. I agree in principle—but what's also a strength is being able to control your reactions, your will.

Anything you don't master will master you. My

reaction to wasted or lost time is an emotion I can almost always control now, but for a few years, I struggled. When I lost my cool, it wasn't acceptable to me or to anyone who was unfortunate enough to be involved. It's a self-inflicted weakness, and it always embarrassed me. This was a real problem for me and others during my twenties.

The problem originally started when I changed my attitude about time. I didn't have the foresight to imagine having to cope with situations that were out of my control. I didn't realize even capable people (like me, I like to think) can make drastically bad decisions when we're not prepared for an unpredictable change that's completely out of our control.

Then one day I took control of my mind and things changed. It was a beautiful, sunny Texas day, I was driving my BMW roadster down an uncrowded road, cruising along, not too fast, with the convertible top down. Good music was playing on the audio system; I was at peace and in the very best of moods.

When I looked up and realized I'd missed my exit, everything changed in a heartbeat. My smile became a snarl and I could feel my blood pressure soar. My peaceful mood exploded into frustration and anger in a matter of seconds. Missing the exit may sound trivial, but you must understand, by the time I got back on course, I lost time—at least a whole five or ten minutes. I found this totally unacceptable.

As you read this, you're probably laughing at me, but I promise you, I'm not exaggerating my instinctive reaction. What's even more ridiculous is that I'd already

3

been conducting seminars and self-help courses around the country. I'd studied a variety of philosophies, and had participated—as a leader!—in several seminars on self-control. And here I was frustrated and out of control because I had missed my exit.

I got off the highway and detoured through back streets to get back on course. As I drove, I began to think about something I had recently heard. It was still fresh in my mind, and for some reason, it really resonated with me:

If you want to get over a negative situation, begin to find positive things within your negative situation.

I figured, "What the heck? I have nothing else to do; let's see if it works." Though I was awash in my negativity and frustration, I began to look for positive things. At first, I didn't see any, so I began to look for simple things. You could call them simple pleasures.

I remember this next moment so clearly, it could have been yesterday. As I drove up to a red light and stopped, I looked at a car turning toward me from the side street. The driver was smiling, a wide, ecstatic grin. I said to myself, "If I hadn't missed my exit, I would never have seen that great grin."

Instantly, like magic, my frustration vanished. I thought, "Man, this is cool." And when the light turned green, I realized the light wasn't your normal green. The light glowed with a brilliant, rich, fluorescent green. And I thought to myself, "That's the most phenomenal green light I have ever seen. If I hadn't missed my exit, I would never have been able to experience this beautiful green light."

Now I must admit all of this was totally out of character for me, but it worked. I began to feel excited, almost as if I were in a competition to find positive things. It was fun!

I'd made a conscious decision to mentally master my out-of-control, overreacting battle against wasted time. Since that moment with the grin and the green light, I've only blown my top over lost time a couple of times. That doesn't mean I've mellowed to the point where it doesn't bother me. Of course, it does! I just control my thoughts, my willpower, and practice my mental strength.

Every individual has the ability to consciously decide whether to master a situation or to be mastered by it. Every individual also has the ability to decide how long he or she chooses to either master or be mastered by a situation.

There is a time and a season for everything. It is very important that you also understand every season will and must come to an end. As I conduct self-development training and seminars around the world, it amazes me to find only 10 percent of most individuals' mental battles are caused by the situation. 90 percent of their struggles are caused by their inability to move on and simply let go of the problem, the habit, or whatever needs to be in the past. I find it difficult to watch a person wrestle with something that would immediately disappear if they could just simply let it go. It drives me crazy to see an individual be overwhelmed and mastered by a ridiculously simple situation, and I find it hard to be in their presence.

I'm working on my shortcoming of patience in this case, too, and I know soon I'll be more accepting of their idiotic reactions. But until I succeed in overcoming my aggravation at their bone-headed obtuseness, there are quite a few wonderful people whom I avoid because they, unfortunately, choose to be mastered by preposterous situations. To me, this is a form of mental bankruptcy.

For instance, how can two otherwise loving individuals be willing to have their marriage come to an end because they can't agree on whether the toilet paper roll should be hung with the paper over or under the roll? How could a person be a loving wife and mother one moment and the next moment be booked for homicide because road rage made her lose her mind?

Okay, I admit I made these up. Toilet paper has probably never been the cause of any divorce (except during the pandemic), and road rage can never be an acceptable alibi for murder.

But let's agree on this concept: Good people make bad decisions when they forfeit the right to master an obstacle or adversity and instead allow it to master them. It's said that you can always measure the character of a person by the size of the obstacle it takes to overcome him.

Good people become murderers every day—and good people are murdered every day—because of individuals who simply are not in control of their emotions. Think about it: How many people do you think are dead or in prison either because of their middle finger or someone else's middle finger? I don't truly know the answer, but isn't it ridiculous to think that a middle finger could cause an individual's rage to escalate to the point of deadly force? How hard would it be for most people to prepare or train themselves never to allow someone else's physical gestures to control them?

These days, different political preferences have caused apparently irreparable rifts in families and between friends. Are people going to avoid their best friend or brother forever because a yard sign, a comment, or a social media post made them blow up? Just because the country is not as bipartisan as it should be is no reason they can't have the generosity, love, and the will to accept different viewpoints. They can summon a smile as they work on negative reactions and keep their blood pressure under control.

What and who push your buttons and have the ability to cause you to lose control and step out of your character? When you hear the words "lose control," it's probably a natural instinct to think of individuals who are literally out of their minds or crazy. We hear these phrases all the time: "He really went off the deep end this time," "She just lost it," or "He just flipped." These are extreme examples, but we lose control every day without having the excuse of real mental illness.

Individuals who are not conscious of the fact that they are capable of losing control will adopt the habit of losing control. And one who adopts the habit of losing control creates the lifestyle of one who's out of control.

On the positive side, control can be regained. If you ever said, "I can't believe I just said that," or "I apologize for snapping like that," you were actively regaining control. You were making a deposit into your mental wealth account, and the next time around, it'll be even easier to recover your equilibrium.

Are you conscious of the moments where you're less in control, and willing to clearly accept and admit that you're being mastered?

I was once told that you should manage your weaknesses and master your strengths. I'm not saying we can ever be successful at mastering all of our emotions and every situation, but I am saying every successful step forward is a step toward being the master rather than being mastered. I believe if you practice mastering the basics—or what some would call the minor things in life—you are actively positioning yourself to avoid potential disasters. You are developing your will.

Is it possible to be in control in a very intense and heated situation? Absolutely! Let me give you an example.

Have you ever seen an NFL highlight special? It's like an R-rated version of a Super Bowl highlight special; there's no editing, and you can clearly hear everything the football players are saying on and off the field. It's mind-boggling to see a 300-pound man tackle another 300-pound man on the field, watch them both crash down onto the ground with one on top of the other, faces distorted with rage, screaming insults and yelling into each other's faces, close enough to feel the spit. Then the referee blows his whistle, and bam, it's all over. They help each other up, perhaps even with a friendly pat, and walk back to their huddles as though the tackle never happened.

How can a warrior type of guy, someone who is so revved up with total focus and intense energy, filled with competitive emotions, regain complete emotional, physical, and mental control in a nanosecond, just with a signal?

Do you know what's really crazy? That same football player with the willpower and discipline to walk away from someone who's spitting in his face and screaming insults while slamming him to the ground is the same guy who gets arrested the next week for a bar fight with a drunken football fan who calls him a loser.

Could this be the same person? And by the way, aren't legal penalties for breaking a drunken loudmouth's head more severe than a ten-yard penalty from the NFL?

For years, these players have been mentally conditioned by their coaches; they completely understand that the consequences and penalties coming from uncontrollable behavior on the field are simply not worth the risk. The mental conditioning is at least as important as the physical training. Their results speak for themselves. Many of them just don't carry this discipline out into the rest of their lives. They don't see it as an asset they can use wherever they are—a form of mental wealth.

The questions to ask yourself are these:

Who's coaching you to understand the adversities you will face in the real world?

Who's teaching you how to evaluate the risks?

Who's teaching you how to control your mind and develop your will?

Who are your mentors?

Let me repeat: We are the only creatures with the gift of self-will. This means that we do possess the capacity and the power to control our minds. We can develop the mental wealth to be able to afford our dreams, and the mental strength to keep us on track. We just need to find the coaches and mentors to help us reach our potential.

Our minds are terrible things to waste. Please don't waste yours.

Author's Notes

My first childhood memory was living with my mother and brothers in a homeless shelter for battered women. As a teenager, I hung out with a tough group of friends and even owned a gun because it was expected of me. My path seemed predetermined— and then suddenly a friend was murdered and I did an  about-face, using my self-will for the first time.

I began to build my mental strength and mental wealth, and I changed my life. I got a job, went to college, married my sweetheart, wrote a best-selling book, *From the Hood to Doing Good*, started my journey to wealth, and began speaking around the world. I coached, mentored, and founded philanthropies. As CEO and President of Wimbrey Training Systems, I oversee and create programs for personal development, wealth and career management, sales training, and speaker instruction.

I've also been a TV and radio host, and the co-author of several additional books, *Multiple Streams of Inspiration, Conversations on Success, Break Through, P.U.S.H. (Push Until Success Happens)*.

In my book, *Building a Millionaire Mindset,* I focus on entrepreneurial success and lay out a simple "building block" approach to growing your business to the million-dollar level. Each chapter deals with a single task you must complete before you move on to the next one, and I share my insights and give you tools to help you make it happen.

My wife and best friend, Crystal, and I live a busy and fulfilling life in Southlake, Texas with our three wonderful children—our daughters Psalms and Hannah, and our son, Honor.

Contact Information

Johnny D. Wimbrey

Master Motivation/Success Trainer
Most Requested Topics:
Motivation/Keynote
Overcoming Adversity
Youth Enrichment
Leadership/Sales
www.JohnnyWimbrey.com

 @Wimbrey

 Wimbrey

 @Wimbrey

 JohnnyWimbrey

14

The First Bill You Pay Is the One You Owe Yourself

Eric Cabrera

So, you have wants and desires. You're ready to take life to the next level. You might crave a new car, a house, more money, a loving spouse, or to improve an important relationship. Let me ask you: *What have you done to achieve these things?*

Now is the time to be honest with yourself.

Up until now, the chances are that you've acted like most of the people in the world, and you haven't seized the opportunity to better yourself, taken a chance on yourself, or stepped out of your comfort zone to grab what you desire. You haven't done so because, before you even took the first step, you counted yourself out.

You count yourself out because of a negative physical or emotional experience from your past. While you've dreamed of taking life to the next level, you don't have the hunger—and faith in yourself—to do it. Instead, your faith is in your own excuses and what other people say and think about you. You value other people's opinion of you more than you value yourself and your own capabilities. You don't entirely believe you deserve your heart's desire.

You have allowed your beliefs to create a false sense of fear.

So many of you are stuck in this identical cycle because of your past. You all have had challenges, obstacles, stories of loss, and failures in your lives, some that have continued for years and some that are very short-lived. Too many people are stuck because you don't love yourself enough to know your own true value.

> *Knowing your self-worth gives you the strength and confidence to choose opportunities to improve your life or someone else's and pass on those that won't.*

Too many of us don't fully recognize our self-worth.

Self-worth is a reflection of our overall vision of ourselves, built up over our lifetime, and always evolving. It's a combination of who we think we are, what we truly believe we deserve, and our faith in our own abilities. Self-worth is also affected by our innate belief system—for example, whether we automatically think and react positively or negatively.

16

When I was younger, I had no self-worth. I grew up in New York in a very dysfunctional household. During my childhood, being dragged out of bed and kicked around was routine for me. My mother loved me and was horrified by my father's abuse, but she was unable to protect me and in no position to leave the marriage. She had multiple sclerosis and breast cancer and was totally reliant on my father for support.

When I was eight years old, my father pushed me through a wall, breaking my collarbone and dislocating my shoulder. I remember holding back my tears, focusing my pain as energy to keep from crying because I knew if I cried, he beat me even harder.

As a young adult I recognized and overcame the effects of my childhood environment. I was able to recognize that my knee-jerk reactions impacted my relationships with others. For example, when my wife and I argued early in our marriage, any tears she might shed only made me angrier.

When I finally dug down enough to understand the trigger, I was so relieved: My anger at her tears was because I could never cry as a boy, no matter what abuse I suffered. That insight took years of hard work and awareness. I finally realized she had every right to cry, and I apologized for all the times I'd been mad.

But when I was still a boy, the years of childhood abuse just left me hating who I was and always feeling angry, scared, and alone.

Worst of all, I felt worthless. I truly believed I was.

On July 7, 1988, I was 12 years old. My father had just come home and I was rushing up the stairs to hide

17

in my room and avoid him. He ordered me to come back downstairs, and I hesitated in terror of what might happen. As I turned around, he was rushing up the stairs, headed right at me. I crouched down to protect myself as he pounded me with his fists. When he was finally tired of punching, he kicked me down the flight of stairs and went to his bedroom.

When I managed to get to my feet, everything seemed to move in slow motion. My nose was bleeding and my body hurt all over. My mother was standing in front of me, crying and saying something, but I couldn't understand her through the ringing in my ears. I looked down the hallway into the kitchen, thinking *I can get a knife and kill him when he passes out, or I can walk out the front door and never come back.* Thank God, I chose to walk out the door. I left with nothing, not even shoes on my feet.

When I reflect on that pivotal moment, I now recognize I left that house with a lot more than just my bare feet. I left with a fresh start to a new life. I left with strength, dignity, courage, and self-respect. I left with a smidgen of self-worth. I left with all those things and didn't even know it at the time. It took years to figure out that I chose *me!*

I made the choice to change my life when I decided *I am worth more than this and I deserve a better life,* left home, and never returned. Other than staying in touch with my mother and brother, I severed all ties and was on my own as a teenager.

Life didn't suddenly take a sunny path, however, just because I left home. I spent the next five years angry and making bad choices, often homeless, hanging out in the wrong places, and surrounding myself with people who were going nowhere. I was headed to the exact same nowhere with them.

When I was 17, a terrifying experience I had while running drugs made me realize this was not the lifestyle for me. I knew I needed to get out of New York, so that night I bought a one-way plane ticket to Florida on the first flight out the next morning.

When I left New York with exactly $306 in my pocket, I had never been to Florida, didn't know anyone, and didn't have a place to stay. That didn't bother me, because I had been homeless off and on, and I knew Florida would at least be warmer than New York. On my first night in Orlando, I found a room to rent. A week later, I landed a job as a stock boy in a department store.

Soon after, while I was listening to an older gentleman who was telling me his life story (that guy loved to talk), I heard words that shook my soul to the core: *I can be a victim or a conqueror, but I love myself too much to be a victim, and I know my value. Do you know **yours**?*

Something inside me shifted. I knew my mindset wasn't that of a victim, but then I realized it definitely wasn't a conqueror's, either. Instead, it was stuck in the middle, in a no-man's-land. Plenty of my history could entitle me to play the victim card, but even at 17, I knew that's exactly what it was—just old history. It was behind me. I didn't need to be stuck anymore. My beatings were the result of my father's issues, not mine.

19

What happened wasn't my fault and I didn't need to bear the burden of his problems.

As time went on, I realized my responsibility is to love myself and know my self-worth, and that's a prerequisite for living a joyful life. My happiness is just that—*my* happiness—no one else's. After absorbing that bit of wisdom, I was able to figure out that my past doesn't dictate my future: *Where I've been doesn't control where I'm going.* I needed to start loving myself and learn my value and self-worth. I looked back at all of life's opportunities I had missed because I was just existing, not living. I was dead inside. I was blind and unable to see the greatness inside me because it was buried in the grave of darkness caused by the shadows of my past.

Years of hard work and self-improvement followed this initial insight.

You can learn from history's greatest people, including Abraham Lincoln, Albert Einstein, Martin Luther King Jr., and Thomas Jefferson, but some of the most valuable lessons in life will come from your own history.

Look at your history. Look at every failure, every loss, every setback, and I guarantee you can find a lesson. The lesson may not be *what to do* because *what not to do* can be equally valuable. When you look back, tell yourself you're thankful for these experiences because you will find positive lessons in them.

I promise you if you look for the positives, you will find them! This will allow you to look at each failure as a step closer to success, every loss as a gain, every setback as a catalyst to advancement.

Finding positive lessons helps you appreciate and celebrate those failures, losses, setbacks, and past events. This shifts your mind to start thinking positively, the first step to loving yourself enough to build your self-worth.

As your self-worth grows, as you develop a favorable opinion of yourself, you'll also start to build unshakeable faith in yourself. You are not a prisoner of your past or anyone else's. Look at your past as a lesson, not as a life sentence! You'll realize you don't have to live in the past and that you can live today with tomorrow in mind.

I'm in my early forties, retired from my first career, and living in Colorado. One morning my phone rang; it was my aunt calling to say my father had a stroke. I called the hospital and learned my father was on a ventilator, unable to breathe on his own because of brain damage. I got on a plane to see him; I felt it was the right thing to do.

I talked to him for the first time in more than 30 years, and I forgave him for everything that happened and for everything he did to me. I could forgive him because I love myself and I have a strong understanding of my self-worth. I am now able to find so many valuable lessons after many years of living scared, angry, sad, unloved, and feeling completely worthless. After I thanked him, he was taken off life support, and I held his hand until he took his last breath.

Because I know the value of my self-worth, I was able to handle my father's death in the way I did. My faith in myself doesn't depend on his or anyone else's

21

opinion. Your faith in yourself should be based on *your* opinion and yours alone.

I learned to change my mindset to match the desires of my heart by changing my outlook, and by speaking positively, not negatively. There is so much power in the spoken word. You should speak positively and as if the desires of your heart have already manifested. Set short-term and long-term goals. Set goals so high that it makes you feel uncomfortable saying them out loud. Set goals that most would see as unobtainable.

Everything that happens to you, your whole situation, is a product of what you believe. If things aren't working out, it is because you *believe* they won't. Your past has created such a fear inside of you that you don't believe in yourself. You are living your life to please others based on the fear of your past and what others think. Do not settle for a life based on fear.

Spend more time on yourself, and spend more time learning the value of your self-worth. You owe it to yourself, and that is the first bill you should pay. (Well, after you pay your mortgage, or you'll end up homeless!) You probably don't realize it, but you're financing a way of life, and you're using your happiness, your self-love, and your self-worth as collateral. Continue down this road and you'll end up broke and broken. When you truly believe and understand the value of your self-worth, you will be able to say *no* to those negative things that prevent you from achieving the God-given greatness that is inside you.

This is *your* story, *your* situation, nobody else's. Take a hard inventory of your strengths and weaknesses.

Identify your key strength. Build and train that strength not just until you get it right, do it until you can't get it wrong. Only then begin working on your weaknesses. Master your craft.

Who cares what other people think or say about you? They're going to think and say it anyway, and they probably already have. Don't sacrifice your greatness because of somebody else's doubts.

Be hungry! Hunger leads to happiness. Do not let anything stand in your way. Be willing to do whatever it takes, but humble enough to learn from others who inspire you and you want to emulate. Be confident in yourself, love yourself.

Self-improvement is limitless. It's a never-ending process and requires constant evaluation of yourself. Prepare yourself for the amazing opportunities life is going to bring you. It doesn't matter what your level of success is. It doesn't matter how big your house is or what kind of car you drive. You need to have a good understanding of who you are, what your purpose is, why you want that big house, that nice car, or that fat bank account. Your net worth is insignificant if you don't have significant self-worth!

Our lives are nothing but opportunities that present themselves in all shapes and sizes, and the size of our lives is limited by how we respond. When you meet someone, that's an opportunity to make a new friend. When a new job becomes available, that's an opportunity to make more money. When someone invites you to dinner, that's an opportunity to spend

23

time with a person you know. When a friend asks you to help them move, that's an opportunity to do good.

Knowing your self-worth gives you the strength and confidence to choose opportunities to improve your life or someone else's and pass on those that won't. The great civil rights leader Whitney M. Young Jr., said, "It is better to be prepared for an opportunity and not have one than to have an opportunity and not be prepared."

When I was finally able to look at my past from a positive perspective and started loving myself, I realized the value of my self-worth. This created powerful energy inside me, and I knew I deserved better for myself, for my future family, and for the community around me (because you always have to give). I had this insatiable hunger to learn and reach my goals of success because I knew I'm worth it! I told myself every day that I was worth it. My self-worth allowed me to accept opportunities without fear.

Not knowing the value of your self-worth will blind you from seeing and accepting great opportunities when they show up in your life. Not knowing your self-worth will allow you to degrade and discount yourself, saying *I can't do that* or *It won't work* rather than seizing the opportunity.

Let's look at it from a positive perspective. What if you *could* do it, and what if it *did* work? When I'm on my deathbed, I would rather be able to say *I'm glad I tried* or *I'm glad I did* instead of *I wish I would've tried.*

You are worth it! Take this opportunity to learn from your past by taking each negative experience and find a lesson in it. Take this opportunity to spend time on yourself, not on things that waste your time. Take this opportunity to invest in yourself by committing to self-improvement. Take this opportunity to make a plan, not excuses. Take this opportunity to set goals and have solid faith in your abilities to achieve them so you can set new and higher goals. Take this opportunity to start saying out loud every single day, *I am worth it, I have a high degree of self-worth, I am worthy of good things, and I love myself and who I am.*

Listen to yourself when you say those words.

I promise you, do these few things and your life will dramatically change. You *are* worth it.

Author's Notes

After I retired as a lieutenant with 23 years of distinguished service in the Fire Department, I moved to Colorado. I dedicate this project to my three sons, Liam, Riley, and Declan. You are my best friends, you are my "WHY." Love, Dad!

As a dedicated entrepreneur, I've built and sold several businesses. I'm also a real estate investor and philanthropist, and serve on the executive board of two nonprofit organizations. Currently, I own two health club chains, and I'm in demand as a motivational speaker.

Contact information

Email: Generalincrease@gmail.com
Website: www.Generationalincrease.com
Instagram: @the_eric_cabrera
Facebook: Eric Cabrera
LinkedIn: @eric-cabrera-9879201b9

Chapter 3

Free Yourself: Live Without Comparisons

Judy Crawford

When I was five years old, I suddenly realized my family was poor. My parents were fighting over money because there wasn't enough to pay the bills, and Dad yelled, "We might have to live on the streets!" The terror of actually becoming homeless shook me to my core. That fight was a pivotal moment in my life, and it changed me forever.

Even at my young age, I had already determined I wasn't going to live the way we did when I grew up—I was going to live differently. I accepted the fact that I didn't have control over my situation as a child, but I absolutely *knew* I'd be able to change my life when I became an adult. I was a big dreamer as a child. I was so introverted and shy that all I had were my thoughts and dreams.

I grew up in East Los Angeles, a poor, Hispanic community a few miles from downtown Los Angeles, in the opposite direction from the beaches. Even though I am Mexican, Hispanic, and Native American, my light-colored complexion came from my paternal grandmother, who was Spanish. My light skin kept me from fitting in with the others, so I didn't have friends and I was often the butt of other children's nasty teasing. Children can be so cruel without knowing what they're saying is mean.

"" *Comparison is truly the death of joy.*

My family was large—five kids—and I am the youngest. We wore clothes from the Salvation Army or hand-me-downs from our older sisters. Every year my sisters and I each got one new dress for the Christmas holidays. That new dress always felt like a celebration, and I was sure it was the best thing ever. No matter how poor we were, I have to say we were always meticulously clean, with our hair done, clothes immaculate, and everything that was supposed to be white was super white. Each one of us always looked very put together.

But I knew my clothes were not new. To this day, I will not walk into a consignment store no matter how high-end the store is, because I just can't bear the thought of wearing someone else's clothes ever again.

I hated going to school because I never felt welcome. Starting in kindergarten, I ran away from school a lot, always heading straight for our house. The first few months, I ran away almost daily, and I somehow managed to find my way home across streets and through at least a mile of rough neighborhood, sort of like a homing pigeon.

When I showed up at the front door the very first time I ran away from kindergarten, my older sister immediately loaded me into the car, drove me back to my classroom, and handed me over to my teacher. I decided I needed a sneakier strategy, so from then on, each time I left school and made it home, I'd wait outside where my family couldn't see me until I thought it was too late in the day for them to drive me back. I remember plotting out my moves so clearly, even now, decades later.

After a few years, my mom lost all patience with my running away from school. At times, I feared she might go off the deep end if I continued, so I finally stopped leaving class and running home from school. I still hated school, though!

My brother was four years older than I was, and he was also being mistreated at school. The few times he had lunch money, someone would steal whatever he had. They'd threaten to punch or hurt him to make him give up his cash. When I was nine, my parents had enough, finally, and said, "It's time for these kids to go to a school where they're not beaten up and don't want to run away." They made the difficult decision to send my brother and me away to live with our oldest sister, 30 or so miles from home.

I was *so* excited to have this new adventure. Moving into a new house, going to a new school with the hope that finally I could find some friends and be happy at school. Up until this point, I despised everything about school.

29

The night we moved in with my big sister, I was wound up and couldn't sleep at all. It was a lot to take in. Instead of sleeping in the dining room at my parents' house, I shared a bedroom with my niece, and we had multiple bathrooms to use. It was a whole new world.

This new world wasn't all sunshine and roses, though. My older sister was having an affair with a very well-off married doctor who gave her an unlimited supply of prescription drugs, keeping her pretty high most of the time. The doctor also supported all of us financially, paying for the house, utilities, food, and most of the family's necessities—just about everything except clothes.

30 I didn't realize until my first day of school that I now lived in a very well-off neighborhood. My circumstances changed from deep poverty to great wealth in an instant, and my life was very, *very* different. I now went to a primarily white school, and even though I was light-skinned, I was asked many times if I was Mexican.

It was a reverse of what happened in my first school in East L.A., where I was often asked if I was white. There I'd always answer, "I'm Spanish, Mexican, and Native American," but the other kids wouldn't believe me.

Asking these questions has never made sense to me and I've never understood why race matters to the people who ask, but it is very obvious this is very important to them. I've never even *thought* to ask anyone about their race or ethnic background. I've always felt it shouldn't matter, that we're all the same—just people.

What overwhelmed me in my new surroundings was the sheer amount of wealth all around me. I was the poor kid in the hand-me-down clothes taking the public bus to school, surrounded by kids with expensive new clothes and riding in the beautiful cars their parents drove. I had never even seen cars like those before!

I realized I was now living at the opposite end of my parents' spectrum. I was surrounded by money. Most of my friends had whatever they wanted because their parents were wealthy.

By the time I reached high school, I had many friends, and they were amazing people. We had a "tribe vibe" going. Though I had a blast with the social part of high school, I still didn't like school itself. My freshman year was a disaster, and I pretty much failed every class, even PE.

My father sat me down and had a talk with me. He told me I had to take school seriously if I wanted to improve my life by going to college and finding a career I loved, one that financially supported me. He finally got through to me, and I decided I was going to do the work and try my best to be a better student. During the next school year, I had much better grades and I was much happier about school.

At this point, I learned all about "comparison," and, oh, my goodness, I suffered because then I couldn't *stop* comparing. I compared my situation, my clothes, my hair, the cars, the houses, myself, my *everything* to everyone else's. I lived this way for years! I was miserable, but I didn't know any better.

In school, I would walk down the hall and say to myself, "She's got great hair and mine is awful," or "Look at her shoes and look at my ugly ones." I compared to the point of sometimes even not wearing shoes to school because I couldn't stop comparing mine to other people's more expensive and better-looking shoes. My logic for going shoeless was simple and hard to argue with: *I can't compare feet because we all have feet!* Inevitably, I would be sent to the office, and they would make me put on my shoes.

I was victimized many times by my own thoughts because I never said nice things to myself. The way I talked to myself was just awful and rude, and I was meaner to myself than anybody else had been or could be.

Things began to change when I took a class in public speaking. For some unknown reason, I allowed myself to become open and vulnerable for my first speech, and I shared how at times I felt defeated by my own thoughts. Not only did I get an A on the speech, but many of the other students also came up to me afterward and told me I helped them to realize they were being their own worst enemy at times.

It was liberating to hear I wasn't the only one having such negative thoughts. I was relieved to learn the private discussions I had in my head were common among people, even the ones I was convinced were full of confidence and had it all together.

At that time, I didn't realize all my experiences would have great meaning when I grew up, and they would impact my life in the business world. Now I've realized I could never have achieved all that I have accomplished if it hadn't been for these painful experiences. When I remember these awkward times in my life, I realize I was not a victim, but a person learning how to adjust and pivot for whatever life throws at me.

Every one of the painful moments has been educational, and I am very grateful to have gone through what I did and come out the other side appreciative rather than bitter. I know I could have very easily gone down the victim path.

As a young adult, I took all of these experiences and applied all of the good I learned about myself and about people. I tried college for one semester, but college just didn't resonate with me at all, and by the time I was 19, I was ready to go out into the real world. Because I could type more than 100 words per minute, my speed and accuracy helped get me in the door of a small law firm where in theory, I was the litigation secretary, but for all practical purposes I was the *everything* girl: answer the phones, type, open mail, make appointments, banking, and make post office runs. I did it all.

I learned everything I could, and after three years, I left for the big leagues—a great job with an exceptionally large law firm in downtown Los Angeles. That's where I met my husband, and life just took off from there. We married, had a daughter a couple of years later, adopted our son soon after that, and off we went.

After we decided to move away from Los Angeles to California's Central Coast, I really hit my stride and started racking up some notable accomplishments, especially in real estate. My career milestones include serving as the president of our town's real estate board, and I led us through the many adjustments we had to make during and after the 2008 market crash. Our town's association stayed financially healthy during my term as president, even in 2009, when we were in the throes of the great recession. I've had great success in almost everything I have done.

As well as working on my professional skills, I invested time, energy, and money into my personal growth. A great therapist/life coach worked with me for the next 10 years, but I didn't stop there. For more than 35 years, I've focused on how to perceive things differently than the way our mind wants us to believe.

I've learned to look at *everything* as a learning experience.

It's incredibly important to me to have a mentor in my life, and my husband has been a great mentor to me. His experience with coaching high school football and mentoring many young men has also been impactful for me. Many of his players come back to either coach alongside him, visit, offer support, or just to say "hi" because he made such a change in their lives. When I see his impact on these young men and its obvious value, it reinforces the importance of mentorship at a young age. Most importantly, I've learned our lives are meant to be learning experiences.

We need to focus on the big picture of what we're learning and doing, and not get caught up in minutiae, negativity, and comparisons.

Comparison is truly the death of joy. Comparing yourself to others will literally kill any joy in you. I learned that lesson late, unfortunately, because I never had a true mentor as a young person. I was an adult before I had a mentor to warn me how destructive what I was doing to myself was and to stop doing it. Once I learned to stop comparing, my life changed, and I found my joy again!

My biggest life lesson was learning to live from a place of *compassionate detachment.* I have compassion for people and situations, but I am detached from the outcome. That is the one thing that has been the most important in my growth.

We can't worry when things go sideways or even just not as we planned. I lived my life with worry for far too long, until finally, I realized worrying is a waste of time and energy. When I understood I don't have any control over the outcome, no matter *how* much I worry, life became so much easier. Accepting that concept has helped me tremendously in life, and especially in business.

I love to help others see that they can have the life they've always wanted and dreamed of by eliminating worry and living their lives free of comparison.

35

Author's Notes

My life is going amazingly well. Real estate has been very good to me and I'm transitioning into retirement with a leadership role in my new business venture in the technology field.

More than 20 years ago, my husband, Tom, and I decided the big city life wasn't for us, and we moved to the beautiful Santa Ynez Valley in Santa Barbara County. We love the pace and quality of life here on the Central Coast of California. Our daughter, Kelley, lives in Sweden, and our son, George, his wife, Maudia, and our two grandkids, Beau and Gianna (GG), reside close by.

Contact Information

Email:	judy@judycrawford.com
Website:	www.judycrawford.com
Facebook:	www.facebook.com/judy.crawford.106/
Instagram:	judymcrawford

Chapter 4

Your Outlook Determines Your Outcome

Bjorn "Beez" Hendricks

Fear is not real. The only place that fear can exist is in our thoughts of the future. It is the product of our imagination, causing us to fear things that do not at present and may not ever exist. That is near insanity.

Now do not misunderstand me, danger is very real, but fear is a choice.

—Will Smith, as Cypher Raige in *After Earth*

Have you ever dreamed of something you could not attain, no matter how much you wanted it? Maybe you even started working toward your dream, but at some point life interrupted you, and you missed one day, then another, then a week—maybe even two weeks. I am here to tell you that you are *not* alone. *Habit* and *fear* are just two of the many concepts that keep us from achieving our goals. But they all fall into one primary category—mindset.

Mindset

Your outlook determines your outcome. Fear is a mental construct that holds us back from achieving so much. We often say negative things to frighten ourselves:

What if it doesn't work out?

It's too difficult for me!

If I don't try, I won't fail.

It particularly hurts me when I hear people say that last sentence. They're forgetting that if they don't try, they will *never* succeed.

> " The epitome of mental wealth is always learning and trying to improve.

Every one of these statements is a figment of our imagination, our own creation. *We* put those ideas into our own heads. *We* let those ideas fester and grow. Most of us eventually let our fear prevent us from taking the first (or next) step on our path of greatness. We are allowing an imaginary construct to define our journey and our destiny.

A concept I regularly promote to my students is the ability to *unlearn* and then *relearn*, which can be a daunting task, but is vital to our growth. While we are the sum of our experiences at this moment, it doesn't mean our past must define our future. If we open our minds to thinking from a different perspective, we open ourselves to limitless possibilities.

Our mindset matters

You may have heard the rumor that Charles Holland Duell, the former Commissioner of the U.S. Patent Office, said more than 100 years ago, *Everything that can be invented has already been invented.*

The rumor has been debunked and attributed to an 1899 edition of *Punch Magazine* where someone else was quoted. However, let's seriously look at those words. They were said before airplanes were invented—or the television! Definitely before computers. Primitive cars were just being produced. That is a small example of the power of mindset and how perception can change the world.

Imagine if such a narrow-minded belief had been commonplace at the time. The wonders of the 20th century that paved the way for how we live our lives may have never come to fruition. We should always tell ourselves *anything* is possible! We have so much we can achieve in our short existence, and it *all* starts with having the correct mindset to believe we *can* do it.

Why?

When I was presented with the opportunity to contribute to this book, I was equally elated and empowered. The project forced me to sit down and have an internal conversation with my authentic self. I asked myself, *What does mental wealth really mean to me?*

You may have heard the saying: *Success is when opportunity meets preparation.* To me, it's a little more complex: *Success is when opportunity meets preparation and speed!* What do I mean by that? Well, procrastination is another consequence of our mindset, a result of letting fear control our actions, tell us what we can't do, and literally hold us back.

Let me give you an example of an opportunity presented to me just a few days ago. Les Brown and Johnny Wimbrey spoke at a conference and mentioned an opportunity for the right person to co-author a book on a future project. Before I left the conference, I contacted Johnny's team and submitted my application. After they met with me and heard my background, I was invited to work with them on a book that would be released in 2022. They said it was a shame the deadline had just passed on *The Power of Mental Wealth*, because my expertise would have been a perfect fit.

You could have heard the wheels turning in my head.

40

Many have assumed I was born with the ability to identify turning points in my life—forks in the road—but it's something I've developed with much care over the years. This was definitely one of those forks! I asked, "What would it take to get into *The Power of Mental Wealth?*"

When I was told it would take a miracle, I didn't hesitate to ask for details of the miracle and any problems that might be in my way.

Opportunity: The chance to co-author a book with Les Brown, Johnny Wimbrey, and Heather Monahan. I could *not* pass that up!

Preparation: I'm always seeking and learning information, and it gives me the experience, ability, and confidence to write about my topic at length.

Speed: I was told that the project was wrapping up to go to press, and I'd have no more than three to four days to write my chapter and get it to the editors so they could meet the book launch deadline.

Now ask yourself, what would *you* say if you were told you had three days to write a chapter of an important book? Would you say, "That's not enough time!" Or perhaps say, "I already have other plans I can't change." Or would you just wait until next year?

Since tomorrow is never promised, we must always keep in our mindset that *we can accomplish anything today* rather than waiting for another day. If we don't even try, we definitely will never achieve our goals.

Mindset! This is the start of our accumulation of mental wealth and the power it provides us.

41

So many people spend their health gaining wealth, and then have to spend their wealth to regain their health.
—A.J. Reb Materi, Canadian Catholic clergyman

Defining wealth

If you search online for the meaning of *wealth,* a good definition is from Investopedia: *Wealth measures the value of all the assets of worth owned by a person, community, company, or country.*

Now take a moment and think back carefully. When a discussion has come up about wealth in your past, in what direction does the conversation always seem to veer? I am willing to bet that you said *financial wealth* to yourself just now. Actually, there are five:

Financial wealth: *Money.* Money is, of course, the

most common form of wealth people discuss, but many would argue it is one of the least important.

Physical wealth: *Health.* The state of your physical health is probably the second most common version, yet it's too often overlooked. Many entrepreneurs sacrifice their health only to see its value once they obtain financial wealth. Without health, we can't endure the stress and trials we suffer through as we continue to build our financial wealth.

Time wealth: *Freedom.* My personal favorite. Time wealth is what caused me to leave my six-figure corporate career at Microsoft. Though I was already well on my way in my financial wealth journey, I did not own my time. If my son had a basketball game, or my daughter had a dance recital, I had to beg for my own time back so that I could attend—and it was not always granted.

This even occurs in the world of entrepreneurs who think they have finally reclaimed their time since they "work for themselves." Robert Kyosaki introduces the cash-flow quadrant concept in his book *Rich Dad, Poor Dad.* He explains that we need to stop trading our *time for money*; instead, we should trade *results for money.*

When you're an employee or self-employed, you are typically trading your time for money, but when you move to the business owner or investor quadrants, your results generate the money.

Social Wealth: *Status.* At first glance, you may think status holds the least value, but I challenge you to think again.

In 2020, real estate mogul Grant Cardone

participated in *Undercover Billionaire*, a Discovery channel show. He was dropped in a remote town without his fortune, name, or any resources beyond a beat-up old car and $100, with the challenge of creating a million-dollar business in just 90 days. What do you think was the first thing Grant did as the challenge began? He decided he needed to know who the movers and shakers in the town were because the power of networking is *priceless*. If you are around the right people, the opportunities will flow toward you. Social wealth feeds into every other form of wealth.

Remember this as you read the chapter: *Wealth can be contrasted to income, in that wealth is a stock and income is a flow.* The statement can be seen in either absolute or relative terms. So what term would I use to define mental wealth?

Mental Wealth: *Wisdom*. During my corporate career, when I was trying to improve operations at large firms, I often looked at different types of process management methodologies, and found knowledge management was key. Within that field, there is the **DIKW** model/pyramid, which demonstrates how we improve our level of understanding as we add context to data:

Data. A collection of facts in a raw and unorganized form.

Information. Adding the context of *what* (or *who, when, where*) to the data brings us to a higher level of understanding.

Knowledge. As we continue to add context, we now look at the *how*. How is the data relevant to our goals?

43

How can we apply the information to achieve our goals? How does this connect to other information so we can add more value and meaning?

Wisdom. Now we get to the *why*, which is at the top of the DIKW pyramid. First, we answer questions, such as "why do something," and "which course of action is best." At this level, you're moving your knowledge from the previous level into action!

So, if wealth is *stock*, or accumulation of something, and mental wealth equates to *wisdom*, then you can deduce that mental wealth has a lot to do with the accumulation of wisdom. The epitome of mental wealth is always learning and trying to improve.

Wisdom doesn't mean just intelligence or book learning. Wisdom can be as simple as coming to the realization that *fear is not real and only exists in our thoughts of the future.*

Now, do you see where I'm going with this?

Growth

When it comes to creating financial wealth in this world, there are only three major financial vehicles you can use:

Real estate. A tried-and-true method that stands the test of time. Some of the richest people in history amassed their wealth by accumulating property.

The financial markets. Includes stocks and the like, and is another great way to diversify your portfolio.

Building a business. Where I spend most of my efforts. You can create far more wealth for yourself when *you're* the one who started the business—much more so than investing in someone else's business.

We can see now that amassing wealth in finance is similar to amassing mental wealth. Look at real estate for an analogy: While fix-and-flips are great for short-term profit, it's the buy-and-hold strategy that creates generational wealth.

We need to use the buy-and-hold strategy when acquiring wisdom. We should keep investing in our minds by attaining more knowledge, eventually transition this knowledge into wisdom, and aim to diversify the knowledge we acquire. We will always grow our mental wealth faster when we shift our thinking and understand we are *investing in ourselves!*

As any good financial planner will tell us, it's important to periodically evaluate our portfolio to see what can be strengthened. The same goes for our minds.

Credit

Because we are comparing mental and financial wealth, let's pivot slightly to discuss credit.

The power and use of credit are fundamental to the Business Builders methodology I developed, which allows you to identify, start, and scale multiple autonomous businesses, where you steer the process instead of operating within it. Credit is vital to this methodology, as it can be used to start and grow any business.

I also preach about the importance of business credit over personal credit. While that concept is worth a separate chapter, you should also understand your personal credit is still necessary as a personal guarantee

(PG) when you apply for business credit, so don't neglect your personal credit profile.

Credit utilization is just the measure of how much of your available credit you currently use across all your accounts. It makes up 30% of your credit score, second only to your payment history, which is 35% of your score.

It's often said that you should keep your utilization below 30%. That's not a bad percentage, but it doesn't help your credit score. Let's look at this in more detail.

Let's say you have five credit cards with different credit limits. Let's also say that one of those cards has a $2,000 credit limit and the total sum of your credit card limits is $10,000. If you charged $2,000 on that first card, you have utilized 100% of the credit limit on that card. That scenario affects your relationship with that specific credit card issuer, and *may* even lead to the company decreasing your credit limit or canceling your card.

If all your other cards have zero balances, you are still using 20% of your *total* credit limit. It's not bad, but it doesn't increase your score. To have a *positive* effect on your credit score, you need to keep your credit utilization score below 10%; 2%-6% is the optimum goal.

So, what does any of this have to do with the power of mental wealth?

As I have matured over the years, I have realized it's not enough for me to be passive with my mind or body. When I was in my 20s, if I had stopped lifting weights for a month, my body probably wouldn't have changed much. At my current age, if I stop working out for a week, I feel as though I've aged five years and my flab comes back exponentially.

When it comes to your mind, it's the same scenario. As time goes on, it becomes even more urgent for you to nurture your mental wealth. It's not enough to try to just avoid stress or even to simply remove toxicity from your life. The *real* secret is to actively take steps to improve your mind and change your life for the better.

Unlearn and relearn

If you ever wanted to become an entrepreneur and gain the time freedom I value, one of the best ways to unlearn and relearn is to relate your entrepreneurial journey to your college experience. Ask yourself:

Why are so many of us willing to live as starving college students for four or more years on the hope of eventually making a middle-class salary? But why, after starting a business with substantially more potential income, are we ready to quit in a few months because we aren't rich yet?

47

This question opens our minds to a different perspective. Our lives are not a reflection of the events that happen to us, but a reflection of how we *react* to those events!

We control our destiny! We hold the power to live the life we want, but we must be willing to make certain changes. And it all starts with the mental wealth we accumulate.

Author's Notes

My corporate career focused on information technology management and strategic consultancies, working with Fortune 500 companies, including Accenture and Microsoft, plus several major government agencies. Over the last several years, I made the shift to developing and launching my own multi-million-dollar companies.

Now I'm a successful entrepreneur, known widely for having coined the more powerful and strategic term *Business Builder* to replace *serial entrepreneur*. I'm also known for teaching the Business-Builder methodology to hundreds of students through my Business Builders Institute (BBI) where we focus on financial literacy and ways to improve access to capital. My students have launched many successful, high-earning businesses.

Because my businesses have expanded into multiple service-based niches, I've earned the title of Business Builder Beez. My companies include Capital Beez (financial literacy and business funding); SellerKai (e-commerce supply chain management); Domani Digital (digital marketing); Dominicus Motors (luxury and exotic vehicle rentals and sales); Aytak Solutions (global recruitment and talent acquisition); The Business Builders Institute (entrepreneur education and mentorship); and more.

I'm always passionate about giving back to my community through education on financial literacy, with a focus on building generational wealth. This passion has led me to create HIVE, a social coalition of leaders who work together to improve our communities. I've also co-founded The BAG, Inc. *(Building Assets Generationally)*, a nonprofit focused on helping youth in underserved communities nationwide.

I was born in Jamaica into humble circumstances and grew up in New York. I attended the University of Central Florida, graduating with a degree in Management Information Systems and Computer Science. I hold multiple certifications including Lean IT Expert, CISSP, ITIL Expert, PRINCE 2, and Lean Six Sigma. I'm fluent in Spanish and Mandarin, and enjoy traveling the globe.

I live in Fort Lauderdale, Florida with my amazing four children, Damani, 17, Dominic, 14, and twins Kai and Katya, 7. They are truly the *why* behind all that I do.

49

Contact Information

Email:	Info@thebusinessbuilders.training
Facebook:	BusinessBuilderBeez
Instagram:	@BusinessBuilderBeez
Twitter:	@12figurebeez
Websites:	sellerkai.com
	aytaksolutions.com
	getdomani.digital
	thebusinessbuilders.training
	capitalbeez.com
	dominicusmotors.com

Chapter 5

Listen With Confidence

Heather Monahan

I have trained myself to listen. I'm not saying listening is easy or that it comes naturally to me; it definitely does not. I've trained myself to listen because I've learned a powerful fact: When people feel they are really and truly heard, the dopamine in their brain activates and they begin to feel happier. When people feel cheerful, they are more likely to work in harmony to find a solution.

Listening also signals respect, and respect can mean everything to some people.

A couple of years ago, I was called into a meeting at my son's school to address an issue with his behavior. While meetings like these are never fun, they have taught me a tremendous amount about dealing with adversity and growing as a person.

When you walk into a meeting, especially one that might become adversarial, it's easy to let your emotions get the better of you. There is no place for emotion in meetings; the one who shows emotion is the one who loses. I work to calm my breathing and focus on my strategy.

My strategy is to always let the other party "empty their cup" first. Once you do this, you have information to work from, and information empowers you. Heading into a meeting with your guns blazing or your mind filled with assumptions will leave you upset in the end. Very rarely will be you happy with the outcome.

> *There is no place for emotion in meetings; the one who shows emotion is the one who loses.*

I calmed myself, sat down, and did not speak.

Remaining calm and not speaking is not easy. It takes practice and discipline, but when you have a goal in mind, employing the right strategy is key to yielding the result you want. I let the school officials share their position, give me their opinions, and talk as much as they wanted to. People like to hear themselves talk. That is a fact of life. Let them. Let them feel heard. Gain information and position yourself to be empowered; it works every single time.

I could sense my cheeks getting hot. At this point in my life, very rarely do I allow myself to get emotional, with the sole exception of issues around my son, Dylan.

The people in our lives who mean the most to us always have the power to put us in very emotional states in trying times. I forced myself to remain calm and quiet.

Starting the meeting by absorbing all the information the other party has to share puts you in a position of power. I recommend this approach whenever you are walking into a difficult negotiation or meeting. When you enter a similar meeting where there is a potential challenge or disagreement, set yourself up for success by encouraging them to talk by asking them for their thoughts or opinions. Repeat back some of what they say; it helps to keep communication clear and let them know you have been actively listening. Don't say, "I hear you," though, because it does not mean you're listening. It's just an acknowledgment, and the phrase is trite and over-used.

At my school meeting, I listened with courtesy, with confidence, without defensiveness, and with encouraging questions. When they were finished, I was ready to begin.

My goal for this meeting was to ensure my son would be set up for success after I left the office that day. Now that I had heard their position, I was able to clearly see the path for me to achieve my goal. There are a number of ways to arrive at that outcome. It is up to us to see the dots and connect them in the best way possible. I saw the dots, and as I began speaking and asking follow-up questions, I began connecting them. Prior to walking into that meeting, I didn't know exactly what the solution would be, but I did know we could find one.

I started with the first observation from one of the teachers, that Dylan had responded aggressively to a specific situation while he was in her class. What struck me as odd was the teachers hadn't discussed or even alluded to the original situation that ignited this chain reaction with my son. *I* knew what the situation was because I had talked with my son in preparation for this meeting.

That looked like a good dot to connect, so I said something to the effect of, "When we began this conversation today, you started with an example of my son acting aggressively. Can you tell me, in your opinion, what elicited that reaction?"

I was confident and relaxed, because I already knew the answer, and asking her the question forced her to own the facts. Asking questions is an extremely powerful tactic. Asking questions you already know the answer to is an even more powerful tactic. The teacher explained that another boy had said something very cruel about my son on a public school forum.

Asking follow-up questions is a powerful course of action, so I said calmly, "Can we please pause for a moment, because I want to point out that *I'd* feel very angry if a peer of mine did that. Is that behavior allowed at school?".

Of course, mean-spirited behavior is not allowed at school, and she agreed that it was an issue. Next, I asked, "How do you think Dylan could have handled it better?"

"He should have called a teacher for help," she said.

That was my opening. Using an opportunity to gain knowledge and then finding ways to have the other person share their opinions allows you to connect the dots.

My logical follow-up question was, "How often *do* fifth-grade boys tell the teacher on each other?"

His teacher admitted, "I don't see that happen often, but I really wish that kids would tell me instead of handling it themselves." That gave me the opportunity to share information with her that she didn't know.

I explained, "We've worked with Dylan to learn to stand up for himself so that he's equipped to handle problems when there isn't a teacher or adult around. It's a strategy that we've worked on for a year. We all know that as we grow, our strategies and abilities evolve and develop. In theory, some things may work, but in reality often different and more realistic tactics or strategies are needed."

The teachers knew I had listened to them with respect, and they listened to me in turn. There wasn't a hint of adversarial attitude or negativity, and we all showed some empathy.

The meeting went on for an hour. We went back and forth between hearing how the school wanted things to be vs. putting ourselves in my son's shoes and discussing what is more realistic.

In the end, we all left the meeting feeling as though my son's motives and actions were now fully understood. So much good can come from being listened to and understood!

Listening signals respect, and it changes the atmosphere in the room. Especially if the others are criticizing you, *listen*. Don't be defensive—just listen. When I said my cheeks were getting hot in my school meeting, they were flaming. My son was being criticized—and by extension, that included me. I sat and listened with respectful confidence, not defensiveness. When it was my turn to talk, the first thing out of my mouth was a question, not a defensive statement. I handled the criticism well by not responding to it and diverted the conversation to problem-solving.

How you deal with criticism is very important, and it leads to a long-term benefit: Handling criticism well will boost your confidence in the long run—and *that's* a game-changer. Confidence is the one thing that changes everything in the environment. When you listen with confidence, you can embrace collaboration and contribute your own ideas.

I wrote the best-selling book, *Confidence Creator,* to share what I've learned on the subject. As a young woman in a male-dominated part of the corporate world, I had to develop confidence quickly to survive, much less thrive.

A good part of my life is now spent helping other people learn confidence. Yes, it can be learned. Building confidence is exactly like training a muscle that can be built up or depleted; it just depends on the actions you take. You always either build your confidence or chip away at it with every action you take. Once you realize that building confidence in yourself is not only attainable but entirely up to you, you're empowered.

You have this.

So, let's take a more confident look at a situation you're dealing with right now, something that isn't going the way you want.

Is it on the wrong track because everyone involved doesn't fully understand the situation?

Is it because *you* don't have enough information?

Listen with confidence. Don't be defensive. Gain the knowledge and insight you need.

Only then, *after* you've listened and asked questions, confidently share your perspective and opinion.

You will find a way to agree on a solution.

There is *always* a solution. It's just up to us to find it.

Author's Notes

As the founder and CEO of Boss in Heels, I am an entrepreneur. I'm also well-known as a confidence expert, keynote and TEDx speaker, and a best-selling author. My recent book, Confidence Creator, shot to number one on Amazon's Business Biography and Business Motivation best-seller lists the first week it was published.

I earned a B.A. in Psychology at Clark University in Worcester, Massachusetts, and began my career as a brand manager at Gallo Wine before I transitioned into broadcasting. After successfully climbing the corporate ladder for nearly 20 years, I was appointed Chief Revenue Officer for Beasley Media Group and was named one of the Most Influential Women in Radio in 2017.

After 14 years of success and continuous advancement, I was unexpectedly fired by another woman. That was one of my lowest moments and forced me to re-evaluate where I was gaining my confidence from. As I began to reflect, I realized that if I was going to start over as a rookie somewhere, I was going to double down on myself. That is when I made the decision to write and self-publish my first book, *Confidence Creator*, and go to work for myself. In 2018, I was named a Limit Breaking Female Founder by Thrive Global. Next, I launched my podcast *Creating Confidence* and landed on the Apple Podcast top 200 list. Then I was named a Top 40 Female Speaker in 2020 by Real Leaders. Today, my clients include Fortune 500 Companies and professional sports franchises, and I help their employees and clients develop confidence in the workplace and on the court.

I'm also very active in my southern Florida community. I was given the honor of receiving the 2015 Glass Ceiling Award from the Florida Women's Conference, recognizing my leadership excellence in the workplace. I'm also a member of Florida International University's Advisory Council, serving as a mentor and leader in the South Florida Community.

My son, Dylan, and I live in Miami.

59

Contact Information

Website: heathermonahan.com
Facebook: Heather Monahan Official
Instagram: @Heather Monahan
Twitter: @_heathermonahan

60

Chapter 6

Beyond the Shame

Kenda Shavon

How do you define *shame*?

The dictionary tells us shame is a painful feeling of humiliation or distress, and I agree. I know that feeling well because I've been living in shame my whole life. As a Black woman in America, I've also had the double jeopardy of feeling invisible.

I've had enough! I'm tired of living in the shadow of shame, and I refuse to be invisible any more. It's time to share my story.

Even before I took my first breath, I was invisible. My mom had an ectopic pregnancy, and when the doctors removed the baby from her fallopian tube, they didn't notice me growing in her uterus at the same time, a very rare occurrence. When my mom was much larger a few months later, the doctors realized she was still pregnant with me, the invisible twin.

Though her doctors didn't think my mom would live if she gave birth to me, her faith was strong, and she was able to carry me almost full term.

My earliest childhood was spent in a small one-bedroom house on Quindaro Boulevard, considered the hood in Kansas City. My dad was pastor of Guiding Star Missionary Baptist Church in that neighborhood. When I was four, my family moved into the parsonage, next door to the church. I remember it as a big, scary-looking old house, more than a hundred years old. Growing up as a pastor's kid was very difficult because we were held to a higher standard than the other kids in the church.

Your past mistakes don't have to define you or your destiny.

Being at that church was a painful experience, for us kids and also for my parents. My dad endured too many heartaches at that church. My brother and I overheard members say terrible things about him. He endured verbal attacks, slander, and almost physical assault.

What affected me the most was my inability to get my dad's attention, for which I always yearned. To him, the church always came first, despite its dysfunction, and I was invisible—he only saw me when I was bad and my actions reflected on him. When I became a teenager, I really rebelled, and I lost my virginity when I was just 16 to a boy I barely knew. Right after I turned 17, I found out I was pregnant. When I finally gathered the courage to tell my dad, he gave me no support. He said he was very disappointed in me, and demanded, "Go in front of the congregation, confess your sins, and apologize."

I knew he wanted me to smooth things over with the congregation, but I refused. "Absolutely not! I don't owe those church people an explanation or apology. *They* don't have a heaven or hell to put me in. The only person I need to ask for forgiveness is God!"

My dad was furious and barely spoke to me the entire time I was pregnant.

Being a teenage mom was *so* hard. My daughter, Alycia, was born on February 7, 1995. I graduated from high school in May, just before I turned 18, and in August I was raped. There was no support for me then, either; I was told to keep my mouth shut and drop the charges.

At barely 18, I was living with the shame of losing my virginity to a boy I barely knew, the shame of being a teenage mom on welfare, and the shame of being raped. By the time I was 19, I was pregnant again. This time I chose to have an abortion, a decision I now regret, but at that time in my life I thought it was best. The abortion added another layer of shame and left me feeling empty inside.

Husband Number One and I were married when I was 20. Three months into the marriage, we were

arguing, my daughter started crying, and he picked her up and actually threw her little toddler body across the room. That was the end of that marriage, and we had it annulled.

I was living on food stamps, welfare, and Section 8 housing, just floundering, having no clue about what to do next. A friend encouraged me to go into nursing, but my parents disagreed. They told me going to school wasn't worthwhile in my case because I had a baby, and they said I should just get a job.

I didn't want to rely on government programs. To care for Alycia the way I wanted, I knew I'd need an excellent job, better than I was qualified for. I enrolled in a licensed practical nurse (LPN) program, to my parents' dismay.

64

School was harder than I'd expected. An instructor actually told me, "You need to go into another profession; you won't make a good nurse." I realized school would be an uphill battle, but I couldn't let one unsupportive teacher decide my fate and determine what God had for me. I toughed it out, graduating as a licensed practical nurse in 1999 and getting my associates degree as a registered nurse in 2000.

Soon after that graduation, I also became pregnant for the third time, but this time I was ready for it and super excited, as was the baby's father. I went from being overjoyed to the trauma of a stillbirth. I had the most horrific, painful experience in my life when I suffered through two days of labor to deliver my perfect one-pound daughter, Caprion, on October 6, 2001.

After I lost Caprion, I became obsessed with having

another baby, and was thrilled when I became pregnant five months later. Since it was our second pregnancy, the father and I thought we should make it official and get married. When I was eight months pregnant, we went to the courthouse, signed the papers, and I was married to Husband Number Two. Because we were just going through the motions for our child, our wedding wasn't a happy celebration.

On December 2, 2002, my beautiful son Julian was born via c-section. His father and I separated in 2004, but our divorce was not final until March 2006.

After my divorce, I reconnected with a man I'd dated years before. This time around I fell in love, and when he proposed, I didn't hesitate. Husband Number Three and I had a destination wedding in Jamaica in October 2008, and it was one of the best days of my life. Sadly, it was probably also the best day of our marriage. I learned the hard way that love alone doesn't guarantee a happily-ever-after relationship.

My time and energy were going into my career instead of my marriage, and my goal was to become a nurse practitioner. After earning my bachelor's degree in nursing in 2008, the next year I went to Research College of Nursing for my master's degree. I also worked at a Kansas City hospital where I experienced constant, overwhelming racism. Several doctors wouldn't speak to any of us Black nurses, which deepened the feeling of invisibility I'd always had as a Black girl growing up. Also, I was insecure about the way I looked, and other nurses often made disparaging comments about my booty and my hair. It was in-your-face racism at its truest form

65

and very stressful to deal with on a daily basis.

Unfortunately, there wasn't much happiness in my marriage to help compensate for the pain at work. We argued constantly. During my 35th birthday party, we both had too much to drink, and he hit me in the face. I was in denial of his violence that time, but when he hit me again months later, I didn't hesitate and called the police. He went to jail briefly and never hit me again.

Despite the challenges and obstacles, I graduated with my Master of Science in nursing on December 15, 2012, when I was 35. It had been a long journey and absolutely worth every bit of the effort.

I was the first person in my family to get a master's degree. Who knew the teenage mom from the hood would be able to accomplish her dream of becoming a nurse practitioner? When everyone told me I couldn't or shouldn't, I didn't let their words stop me.

It turns out I had the inner determination, strength, and resilience to keep pushing forward. Now a major mission of mine is to encourage people—*especially* women—to go after their dreams and not place limitations on themselves.

My career was successful, but my marriage was failing. I was tired of living in Kansas City, tired of all the racism surrounding me, and, frankly, tired of my marriage. In 2015, when a position opened at the VA Hospital in Dallas, Texas, I applied for the job without telling my husband. I waited until I had the job offer before I asked if he'd move to Texas with me and make a fresh start.

My husband said *no*—he was comfortable living in

Kansas and didn't want to leave his mama. Because I recognized how distant we'd become, I accepted the job offer and moved to Dallas alone. I immediately loved the city, finding it friendly and welcoming.

Just a month after I discovered Oak Cliff Bible Fellowship, I was alone in my apartment when I had a sudden spiritual awakening. I repented my sins, gave my life to Christ, and said out loud, "Jesus Christ is Lord, and I believe in my heart that God raised Him from the dead." My dad was a pastor and I'd been baptized and had gone to church my whole life, but I had never been saved before.

I became a member of OCBF and focused on my relationship with Christ as a new woman; old things had passed away and all things became new. I stopped talking to everyone I knew from Kansas City except my family. My friends didn't understand, but I knew this was my time to spend with God.

Then God spoke to me through His word, and I knew I had to move back to Kansas City to try to make it right with my husband. I had been putting my career first before God and my family. I was obedient to what God told me; I walked away from the job, packed all my stuff and moved back to Kansas City to fight for my marriage.

It was too late; I tried to make amends, but he had moved on with someone else, and we were divorced in August 2016. I was 39, and my third marriage had failed. More shame. Two months later, I moved back to Dallas and tried to sweep my past under the rug.

As a Christian, I made a vow not to have sex outside

of marriage, so dating in Dallas as a newly single woman was a hot mess. Finally, I met a tall, dark, and handsome guy on Black People Meet. We exchanged numbers and talked; he also had suffered the death of a child and knew the pain firsthand.

On our first date, he told me I was his wife, but of course, I didn't believe him. All my life I'd been longing for love from my dad, and I'd looked for it in all the wrong places, so I was very skeptical of this gentleman. And he sure was a gentleman! He opened my doors, pumped my gas, washed my car. He took care of me when I got sick. I never dated such a thoughtful man, but I had been hurt so much in the past, I couldn't trust anyone.

When I moved to a new house, I didn't have anyone to help me. As soon as he heard that, my gentleman friend came right over and helped pack up my entire household. That caring and thoughtfulness finally broke down my distrust, and we became a couple. We drove to Kansas City and he asked my dad for my hand in marriage. Dad prayed over us and gave the blessing for our marriage.

On September 22, 2017, I married husband Number Four at the courthouse. I'd kept my vow to God, doing what's right in His eyes, and we had abstained from sex until we were married. To be honest, that's one of the reasons I agreed to marry him so quickly.

In hindsight, I should have waited. We really didn't know each other well and our marriage had a rocky start. We came together still broken, with tons of unresolved baggage, and neither of us had healed from our painful pasts. We tried counseling but it didn't help much. I felt like a loser, filled with more shame because my fourth marriage in shambles, very toxic and draining. Still, I didn't want to give up too easily.

It's easy to find faults in others, but one of the hardest things to do is to look at yourself and see your faults. Finally I took a serious look in the mirror, and I realized *I am the problem.* I realized I couldn't change my husband, I could only change myself.

I loved being a nurse practitioner and didn't want anything to do with being an entrepreneur, but when my new husband introduced me to network marketing, I agreed to go to a conference in Atlanta. There I discovered the company had many successful Black millionaires.

During the conference, the CEO recommended reading *The Parable of the Pipeline.* I realized I hadn't read a book since I'd finished my last degree seven years before. I'd become too complacent and comfortable, I wasn't growing, and I'd become stagnant. It was time for a change.

After I read *The Parable of the Pipeline*, I knew I had to change my life and my way of thinking, and entrepreneurship became an option for me. Reading quickly became a habit; I *knew* I had to gain this knowledge. Joining this network marketing company opened my mind.

At first, my husband and I didn't make much money, but the value of changing my mindset and being around like-minded people, plus they were people who also looked like me, was priceless. I had to get my old programming out of my subconscious mind.

In 2020, COVID hit, and the world shut down. In the middle of the pandemic, I started to stretch myself and get out of my comfort zone. I took real estate courses and started my first business, a real estate investment company, Alluring Heights, LLC. My focus is on generational wealth, because I figured it's time to stop investing in other people's names and leave a legacy for my kids and grandkids.

In 2021, my father showed how he too had grown and changed over the years. He apologized for the way he'd treated me when I was in my teens—and it was in public, in front of his congregation. His loving act tied up some painful loose ends and helped with my healing and growing journey.

The next year, unfortunately, my marriage to husband Number Four finally failed. God revealed to me that I had been living a life of rebellion and lust. I was seeking pleasure over purpose and always picking the wrong men.

Now it's my time to heal and become whole. I'm on a journey to mental and financial freedom, and since success begins from within, it all started with a change in mindset. I've taught myself to speak life affirmations, positive affirmations. *No more living in shame!*

I've moved beyond the shame towards freedom.

I don't need to seek approval, validation, or acceptance from others. I've learned to look to God and look within.

No longer do I feel invisible. Exposing my life still makes me uncomfortable, but if my actions can inspire someone else, then my discomfort is worth it.

If this rebellious teenage mom from the hood can rise above the ashes, *so can you.* Your past mistakes don't have to define you *or* your destiny. I want you to remember you are worthy and you're more than enough.

Your possibilities are endless, with no limitations, no excuses, and no shame. You're alive, you're not invisible. As long as you have breath, it's never too late to make the most of your visions and your dreams.

Now, go! Get what God has for you.

Author's Notes

First and foremost, I am a child of God. I am fearfully and wonderfully made. I walk by faith and not by sight, and resilience is my superpower.

On June 1, 1977, I was born to Lois and Clyde Rice at Bethany Medical Center in Kansas City, Kansas, their only girl and youngest of four.

As a board-certified Family Nurse Practitioner

with more than 20 years of nursing experience, I have an extraordinary commitment to add value to my patients' lives, and I'm dedicated to educating people on kidney disease. Recently, I launched *Lady Nephrology*, a YouTube channel where I discuss topics related to kidney disease. My dream is to eventually open a dialysis clinic.

My life is full of love and rewards beyond the medical world. I've recently moved to Denver, Colorado, and I founded Alluring Heights, LLC, a fast-growing real estate investment company in Chicago. My hobbies include international travel and reading, especially personal development books, though my favorite book of all time is still the Bible. I'm finishing my own book, *Beyond the Shame*, in which I share my healing journey.

The most rewarding aspect of my life is family—

being a mother to my children, Alycia and Julian, and a very proud grandmother to Zyaire. I believe in living life to the fullest. With God's love, I know all things are possible.

Contact information:

Email: ladynephrology@yahoo.com
Facebook: Kenda Shavon
Instagram: Kenda Shavon
LinkedIn: kenda-shavon-033048189
YouTube: Lady Nephrology

Chapter 7

Turn Your Pain Into Power

Gavin Fortuin

Though all of the odds are stacked against them, the young men and women on the poverty-stricken Cape Flats of Cape Town, South Africa, manage to persevere. Working with them and expanding their horizons beyond hustling and crime fills me with humility and respect—and at the same time lifts my sense of self-worth and makes me feel alive.

Don't get me wrong. I don't claim to have it made. While I am headed to a place of significance, my journey still has a long way to go. What matters is I'm on that journey, and this is a big change from 20 years ago.

Then, my life was quite different, and I was in the same place as the young people I'm helping now. My Cape Town community took a very dim view of my teenage self and the company I kept. My friends and I were regularly confronted and questioned by the Neighborhood Watch, civilians who are trained to form a police-assistance league. Often, they had good reason to do so.

I was raised by a single mother, and my longing for a father made me vulnerable to predators. By the time I reached puberty, I'd been sexually molested more than once, including by a man who pretended to be a psychologist and performed various sexual acts on me. I tried to block the incidents out of my mind for years, but not very successfully. I felt self-hatred for letting someone control and use me.

> *Your destination is important, but the person you become along the way is much more valuable.*

By the time I reached high school, I was already creating wholesale havoc. My main objective was to make others sit up and take notice, and the main avenue for this was through mischief and crime. Even at school, gang activity and illegal substances were rife, and whenever anything went down, mine was one of the first names to be mentioned.

Somehow, I realized I shouldn't join an actual gang, but my good sense didn't extend to the company I chose. One of my close friends—we'll call him Denver—did become a gang member, and I was drawn into gang-related conflicts by default. I wasn't officially a gang member, but he and I were tight, and we enjoyed the havoc we wreaked together. Fights were a daily occurrence, and I loved the adrenaline and power that came with them. Denver ended up becoming a member of one of South Africa's most notorious prison and street gangs.

One night in a park, a friend unexpectedly pulled out a revolver and started shooting. I ran for my life as the Neighborhood Watch returned fire, sending a rain of bullets from their semiautomatic pistols past my ears, creating a shower of sparks against a chain-link fence. I ran at full speed, though my adrenaline rush made everything seem to be happening in slow motion.

I should have been hit. Divine intervention protected me as I zigzagged through a jungle gym and sprinted to where I planned to scale the wall to safety. I never made it. Mid-jump, I was tackled from the side, and I spent the rest of the evening at the police station. Reckless as they might seem, episodes like this were par for the course during my teenage years.

I saw myself as beyond redemption, ready to "die a thug," even if not everyone saw me that way. At least one teacher didn't see me as a troublesome thug, but as a young man with potential. Whatever potential she saw in me totally eluded me. She comforted my mother when the principal finally declared me a "menace to society" and expelled me from school.

My mom needed the comforting because she knew she'd lost control of me and was sure things were about to go from bad to worse. Once I was home full-time, all of my time and energy was dedicated to obtaining and using drugs—plus the dishonest and underhanded activity that comes with drugs. I used it in my room, always with a cast of shady characters who saw my house as a safe place to use. Many nights my mom cried herself to sleep while a bunch of us were smoking meth and quaaludes mixed with weed in the next room. Once

I overdosed and only recovered by a miracle.

Shane, my cousin and level-headed best friend who often kept me out of trouble, died after I left high school. We'd been inseparable, and my world fell apart. I was unable to deal with grief and became even more self-destructive.

It seemed as if I was arrested for possession every other week, and often held for an entire weekend in filthy and louse-infested cells. It was clearly just a matter of time before I would be sent to prison.

Mom finally had enough and kicked me out of the house, unwilling to watch me turn into a hardened criminal. She had my younger sister to think of, and my toxic influence was undoubtedly influencing her. At least Mom didn't ban me from the property, so I wasn't completely homeless. I slept outside on a cold concrete slab at the back of the house, my clothes threadbare and my body reeking.

I'm glad Mom finally found the courage to put me out, because the concrete slab is where my life started to turn around. Lying there, I had an epiphany, and I asked myself, *Is this the life I was born for?*

My mom hadn't totally written me off, and when I said that I was ready to leave drugs behind, she helped get me into rehab for the first time. Yes, that wasn't my last treatment center. Relapse often comes with the territory. I benefitted from each stint and have no regrets. Rehab didn't just provide a space to detox and get clean, it was a place where I could start leaving my past behind.

A social worker I met during a rehab stint was the first person with whom I shared the guilt and shame from my past, stories of the people I had hurt, and of those who had damaged me. The healing I got from sharing it all with her was life-changing and made me realize forgiveness is necessary to become free and liberated as a person.

In my case, rehab was also where I began to look to the future, and where I first experienced the influence of positive role models. One of these was an entrepreneur and motivational speaker who, by mere coincidence, happened to be facilitating sessions at two of the rehabs I attended. I don't think he crossed my path twice just by chance.

I owe this man my life. I admired what I saw—confidence, insight, and a passion for helping young people—and I made it my business to stay connected with him. He became my first real mentor, and he coached me in becoming a public speaker and youth practitioner. His aggressive and high-intensity leadership style ensured that I developed a solid foundation so I would have the endurance for future challenges.

My mentor encouraged me to attend conferences, including the Millennium Development Goals and Pan African Leadership forum conferences, to speak at these events, and to ask good questions. He even gave me clothes from his own closet because I had nothing suitable. Walking this journey with him activated my passion, purpose, and assignment on earth.

I learned the value of a mentor and was fortunate enough to find others as I grew and developed as a person. The impact and influence they have on my life shaped the man I am today. Under their guidance, I have learned to put God first in everything. Under their tutelage, I developed an appetite for reading leadership, personal development, and self-help books. They taught me to ask questions to expand my mind and foster a philosophical outlook on life. By watching them, I have seen the heart of activism and the desire to serve the community.

Most of all, they've been good friends to talk with, whether to lift my mood, enlighten me, or inspire me to search deep within myself. While I will not mention them by name here, they know who they are, and I am profoundly grateful for the time, influence, and value they continue to add to the person I am still becoming.

80

Here I'll share three foundational concepts which have changed and improved every aspect of my life. Fully grasping our *identity*, *purpose*, and *vision* are prerequisites to reaching our full potential.

Identity: *Discover who you are*

Truly knowing ourselves becomes our foundation for self-mastery and success. We human beings are the only living creations that don't automatically mature to our fullest potential. A tree will grow until it can't grow any more, and an animal will develop until it can perform at its optimal level. However, we human beings criticize and judge ourselves for past mistakes, despite our infinite intelligence, and we stunt our own growth by punishing ourselves. We must become cognizant of the wealth we possess inside and realize that all we need to do is unfold like a flower in the morning, kissing the sun's rays. A bird's trust is not in the strength of the branch it's sitting on but in its own wings.

You attract who you are is one of the principles I live by. You attract everyone, everything, and situations to yourself like a magnet. The Law of Attraction created the person I am today. The evolution of the power of my thoughts has transformed my life and that of other families forever. When my personal philosophy transitioned from a victim mentality to an abundance mindset, I recognized my thoughts had created my world. I can become whatever I think about.

Our attitude—how we act, treat others, and interact in the world—is an indication of our belief system. Gradually, our character forms at a young age as we absorb every event, interaction, touch, and environment like a sponge. For instance, scientific studies show children growing up with parents who frequently argue and fight have mental health and cognitive problems, among other issues; their brain development is affected.

Awareness of your own insecurities, shortcomings, and limitations is important to recondition your mind to look at life from another viewpoint.

We don't see things as they are,
we see them as we are.

—Anais Nin

Realize that you have the tendency to look and act according to your past experiences and pain. You must demystify bias, culture, traditions, and old habits to embrace the new uncharted frontiers of the future. You have the capacity to use mindfulness to acknowledge who you are now and then change yourself. You can transform like a butterfly going through its metamorphosis.

Being indecisive about who you are will lead to doubt; doubt will create fear. It's imperative to make a decision and draw the map for your journey to success, however you choose to define it. Think of making your decision as if you were starting a surgery. When a surgeon makes the initial incision, he definitively and cleanly makes his cut and doesn't look back.

Use that surgical approach when you make decisions—make it cleanly and don't look back with doubts and regrets. Otherwise, as you flounder and whack away at the decision-making process, reversing your path and changing your mind, you'll become known as untrustworthy. You'll also waste years of your life as you drift around from one direction and path to another, just like a piece of trash in the wind. Your decisions shape your destiny.

82

The only person you are destined to become is the person you decide to be.
—Ralph Waldo Emerson

As you make these conscious decisions about your future and begin moving down your new path, don't haul your dirty baggage from your past along on the trip. Hating and not forgiving others is like drinking poison and wishing someone else will die. Don't allow yourselves to hold onto hatred and resentment; they will consume all the joy inside you, and you'll also be nurturing health risks.

When you continue hating, the person you hate becomes your master and you will never experience true freedom. Cut the umbilical cord of hate and liberate and enlighten your spirit. Forgive, and you will operate from a point of strength and not weakness. In our vulnerabilities lies phenomenal power!

Purpose: ***Identify your gift***

Your gift was given to you by the Divine, and it's something irrevocable that flows naturally through you without effort nor struggle. Your gift does not care how old or rich or poor you are, it will knock on the door of your heart until you decide to answer that call. The day you finally identify your gift and make use of it is the day you are truly born.

When you use your gift, your energy will flow with a higher vibration. That frequency will cause the universe to harmoniously flow to its source, back to you, but increased a hundred-fold. My search for meaning ended when I discovered my gift and purpose by using it and giving it away. My gift is not public speaking, nor is it the ability to facilitate youth programs. My gift is simply an ability to connect with people in a profound way, a way that makes everyone I encounter believe they matter and are special.

Too many people just merely exist, living life so cautiously that they might have not lived at all. They've never experienced true freedom, and for all purposes they're already dead. Don't waste your time with these people. Instead, identify those who are already using gifts similar to your own, and make it your life's mission to study them. Strategically maneuver yourself into their circles of influence and learn how they became successful. Success always leaves clues you can find and link together. Take what you learn and make it authentically your own.

Your next step is to find mentors who are already doing what you want to do and have become masters in their field and industry.

Don't make your goal simply to become "successful." Rather, become a person of *value*. Success will follow, because it will be attracted by the person you become.

Invest in yourself to make yourself more valuable. I practice what I preach, and I'm constantly investing in myself. Personal development is an intrinsic part of my journey to success. Reading books, exercising, eating healthfully, and guarding my heart and mind against toxic people are the habits I cultivate in my daily routine.

Excellence will be attracted by the person you become in your pursuit of unattainable perfection. Your destination is important, but the person you become along the way is much more valuable. Whenever passion fuels your purpose, you will have supernatural energy and a fire that burns within you, one that will never turn into ash.

Nothing worthwhile and great will ever be achieved if you stay within your comfort zone. Pain has a purpose. At some point, you'll suffer from one of two types of pain: the pain of discipline or the pain of regret. Regret is by far the most painful. When you try the unknown and suffer

84

adversity, you'll be introduced to your true self. Use every bit of resistance, use every closed door to shape, prune, polish, and refine your gift to withstand future storms and turbulence.

Find the courage to turn your pain into power.

Vision: *Where are you going?*

When we study many great historical characters, we discover their vision allowed them to succeed desp ite overwhelming odds. When I returned from rehab, writing down my vision in a book was of utmost importance for my journey toward self-discovery and self-mastery.

My ultimate vision is to build a wilderness retreat on thousands of acres of land in Knysna, South Africa, or Alaska in the United States. I envision a self-sustainable, multi-level development/training institution creating employment for the youth of Africa and the world.

When you choose your vision, it will elect everything in your life—your friends, hobbies, income, health, lifestyle, and spouse.

When you imagine your vision, clarity is power, and the clearer you are, the more powerful you will be. Visualize specifically what you want in detail; picture the way it looks, tastes, smells, and feels, and identify the emotions attached to it. Then get to work with that end goal in mind.

Don't allow the limitations of your current situation to become the enemy of *your* vision. Imagination is my secret weapon, and it can be yours. With imagination, you have no ceiling and no limits, and only you can choose how far you want to go.

Author's Notes

In addition to writing, my main focus is Change Agents Developing Youth Leadership (CADY Leadership, for short), an organization I founded in 2018. I'm also a motivational speaker and youth practitioner, and I serve as a consultant to a number of government and non-government organizations on social development and youth-related community issues.

My soon-to-be-published autobiography, *From the Gutters to the Podium: Your Pain Has a Purpose,* goes into more detail about the often-thrilling misadventures of my youth, how I overcame adversity, and the tools I mastered to turn my life around.

I live in Cape Town, South Africa, with my loving and supportive wife, Lynn. We are awaiting the birth of our child.

Contact Information

Email:	gavinsfortuin@gmail.com
Websites:	www.cadyleadership.com
Facebook:	Gavin Fortuin
	CADY Leadership
Instagram:	Gavin Fortuin
	CADY Leadership
LinkedIn:	Gavin Fortuin

Chapter 8

It's Okay to Ask
For Help

Jayln Nicola

I was so sure 2020 would be *my* year. The year before, I'd dedicated my life to the Lord, whom I call Papa, and I knew He would help me with the difficult transition I'd started.

I would never have predicted what happened next—one of the toughest times in history, with a pandemic paralyzing the entire world. For the first couple of months, I was able to stay home with Raquel, my wife, ensuring she was well protected because of her underlying health conditions. All too soon, I received a call from the National Guard that would change my life as I knew it. I was to join the fight against COVID-19 in New York City.

Though I had been deployed around the world during my 20 years in the 101st Airborne and the New York National Guard, my new deployment was definitely more dangerous. I had never been in a situation where the enemy was invisible to the naked eye. I arrived in Manhattan, where I would be working for more than a year, and the first thing I did was go to my office and thank Papa for all He had done for me up until that moment. Then I asked Him to help me through my suffering.

What do I mean by that?

I am a transgender man, and I had decided to live the life I was meant to live. I began my transition in late 2018 with hormones. On the day I received my first testosterone injection, Jennifer Nicola died and Jayln Nicola was born. Not everyone in my immediate circle of friends and family understood, but most were supportive. I had my first surgery scheduled, but unfortunately it had to be postponed because of my COVID-19-related deployments.

> **One of the more subtle additions to my life is learning to forgive myself.**

I battled gender dysphoria for many years. I knew there was something different about me from a very young age. When I was in sixth grade, I was timid and isolated from everyone, and always felt uncomfortable. I didn't want to be just one of the girls. I wanted to be one of the *guys*.

Because I felt I could relate better with the guys, I started hanging with them. Not much later, I started dating girls, and it felt so natural. I met my wife when I was 19, and we have been together ever since. We have four beautiful children and three godchildren.

I had wanted to be in the military since I was a small child; it is all I wanted to be. I enlisted in the Army when I was just eighteen, purely coincidentally on September 11, 2001. Despite the *Don't Ask, Don't Tell* policy in effect for my first ten years, I'd always thrived in the service. While I didn't "tell," I also didn't hide my sexual orientation. As a lesbian, I'd worked my way up to E7, or Master Sergeant, in the New York National Guard. My responsibilities include overseeing our dining halls and inspecting facilities at other bases.

When I deployed to Manhattan to manage food services for COVID-19 patients, no one in my unit knew I had begun my transition to being male. The hormones were seriously affecting me in every way, emotionally as well as physically. Side effects include severe anxiety, weight gain, depression, and hypertension. I felt freaking miserable, ungainly, cranky, and unhappy. My body was changing, but so was my mind.

At the same time, I was working 20 hours a day, trying to do the impossible, responsible for feeding hundreds of infected people, as my transitioning body was fighting me in all sorts of new ways. I never knew how it was going to react. Everything was exacerbated by the fact I was alone, away from my wife and family, my entire support system. When I learned my surgeries had to be postponed because of my deployment, I was devastated—and angry.

My deployments to Iraq and Afghanistan had been stressful, but nothing like this. Of course, the fact that

I was quietly transitioning without any of my troops or superiors knowing and having just three to four hours of sleep per day were the rogue cards in the deck.

There were days I'd say to myself *I can't let my soldiers see me this way* and I'd race to my office so nobody would catch a glimpse of me in crisis. I never asked for help. It's not that I didn't believe in people asking for help; I was always willing and able to help and counsel my troops. I'd mentored and counseled at least 1,000 soldiers since I'd had a suicidal stretch of my own years before, but I would not, *could not,* accept help from anyone else. Whenever I needed someone, I talked myself out of it by convincing myself no one was available.

I'd suck it up and suffer anxiety attacks alone, away from my family, living in a hotel, working unbearable hours a day—right until the day my body and my mind couldn't take it anymore. I almost passed out. My blood pressure was through the roof. I knew I was dying. Finally, I called for one of my soldiers and she came to my aid.

At that point, I was scared, certain I was about to die, but I knew I didn't want to die alone. That's the only thing that made it through my mind at that moment. With my soldier's help, I made it to the hospital, absolutely convinced I was about to make the really big transition.

When I learned my anxiety had triggered a severe panic attack, I realized I'd heard about this from my niece, Ladyann, who'd suffered from debilitating anxiety and depression. She had told me, "Tio, you have no idea what this feels like! It's the worst feeling in the world." Several times she actually said, "I'm going to die from this."

Unfortunately, she was right.

But I didn't know it then. Instead, I'd minimize her pain and say, "Ladyann, stop talking like that!" In my head, I would ask myself *how bad could this really be?* Well, let me tell you, I found out very quickly how bad it was. I regret Ladyann died before I could tell her I finally understood what she was going through.

Once that first COVID-19 deployment was complete, I went home for a month of rest. But all too soon, I received another phone call from the National Guard, and I was placed on orders again. In my second Manhattan COVID-19 deployment, my workload and responsibility grew from responsibility for feeding hundreds of people a day to feeding a few thousand a day. My job was to ensure everyone had four meals to eat. As the numbers grew, so did my anxiety.

Once I realized work-related stress and hormone-triggered anxiety was. my new normal and it wasn't going away, I started researching how I could handle it better. *Finally*, my mind was open to receiving help. I decided to handle it by investing in myself. I really like the way Johnny Wimbrey describes this process in his new book, *Building A Millionaire Mindset*: "***I participated in my own rescue.***"

Once I decided to rescue myself, I was determined to work with the very best at what they do. I made my first promise to myself when I committed to making a very substantial investment, and it's changed my life. I was finally willing to ask myself what I really needed

91

and wanted.

That's why I was receptive when I started to work with Les Brown, one of the best motivational speakers in the world. He gave me the confidence to follow my dreams, helped me recognize some of the obstacles holding me back, and he taught me how to organize my thoughts better. He also started me in a new habit of listening to a variety of other motivational speakers.

One morning I was listening to *The Best Motivational Speeches of 2019* as I exercised, and I'm sure fate intervened to make sure I extended my workout just so I could hear Lisa Nichols' story.

Lisa told listeners that she'd been in an abusive relationship, one so bad that she had lost herself. She finally went to a therapist, who told Lisa she was clinically depressed and should be on medication. Lisa asked the therapist, "May I try something on my own for the next 30 days? I promised if it doesn't work, I'll take the medications you want to give me."

The therapist agreed, and Lisa went home and started taping affirmations all over the walls of her house. She would read each of them every day. At the end of the month, the therapist was amazed at Lisa's results and her improved state of mind. She said to Lisa, "Whatever you did on your own, it's working. May I borrow your method for my patients?"

As I was listening to Lisa speak, I started getting emotional. She spoke about her dad taking her on her "first date." He bought her dinner, and he opened the car door for her. At the end of the evening, Lisa's dad opened the front door of their home for her, but then stopped her from going in the house and said, "Lisa, tonight I took you on your 'first date' so you get to see how you *should* be treated. Now, sweetheart, how you *choose* to get treated, that's going to be on *you*."

At that moment I decided I really needed to change, just for me.

Then I found Mel Robbins and her course, *Mindset Reset*. When I read what she wrote, it felt as though she'd written it just for me: *You are tired of feeling stressed. Life is overwhelming. Ready for some serious change?*

Mel designed a free 35-day program that starts with some self-evaluation, and then she emailed daily exercises I had to complete. That got me started on a positive track. I also began to meditate morning and evening. Sometimes the emotional stress was so powerful I needed to meditate many times throughout the day.

Soon I added Jon Talarico of The Power Voice, who specializes in building relationships. I learned how to find my opportunities and then use a network of connections to build a better life. His theme is "anything is possible."

Now I'm also working with Bob Proctor of The Proctor Gallagher Institute, who helped me find a new purpose in life and wake up each day excited to learn and grow.

I've been learning about investing in the stock market from Darren Winters, and working with Forbes Riley to hone my "pitch."

These powerful and talented individuals have also

taught me how to control my anxiety in ways that give me positive energy. James McNeil has been my mentor for meditation. Meditating twice a day is my goal, and I meet it more and more often. I take care of myself in physical ways, as well. I've been exercising, drinking tons of water, and avoiding alcohol.

One of the more subtle additions to my life is learning to forgive myself. My life has changed for the better. And all because I finally realize that even those of us who help others need to be helped ourselves.

As I reached out, I began realizing what I needed the most and I asked for it: *Papa, please align me with the people who out-think me.*

And sure enough, it's just like Steve Harvey says, "You have not because you ask not." Once I asked, I got.

I asked for mentors and individuals who would hold me accountable for my actions. I was soon aligned with Gary Cowan, a gentleman who would most definitely hold me accountable, no matter how hard I tried to wriggle out of it.

I was also aligned with Kenson Charles, who has become a great friend. Kenson is a straightforward guy who doesn't care if you like him or not. More than once he's told me I need to get my crap together. Kenson is also the guy who pulled me aside and said seriously, "Listen, if you do this, your life will be easier, and it will get better."

I've worked hard to rescue myself, and I've invested a great deal of energy, time, and money. The key takeaway I want to share with you in this chapter is this: *It's okay to ask for help.*

When you suffer in silence, not only is your judgment clouded, but your health is compromised. Even worse—you can actually die from your silence and solitude. Don't allow the gifts you were given to die with you. Have faith that you were meant for more, that you have a purpose you are meant to fulfill. Pull out the champion who is inside of you to push you through the hard times. As Les Brown says, "That's my story and I'm sticking to it."

Author's Notes

As Jennifer Nicola, I was born in Long Island, New York. Now, as Jayln, I reside in New York City with my wife Raquel Rodriguez when I'm not deployed. We have four wonderful children and a beloved godchild. I studied computer engineering and networking at Briarcliff College, and business administration at Colorado Technical University.

The Army and National Guard are a major part of my adult life. I enrolled as a private into the 501st Signal Battalion of the 101st Airborne Brigade, and performed the duties of a Culinary Specialist from 2001 to 2009. After leaving the Army, I continued my military career by enlisting in the New York Army National Guard in 2009, and am still serving to this date as a Food Unit Leader, Sergeant First Class.

My awards and decorations include the Combat Action Badge, Army Commendation Medal with one oak leaf cluster, Iraq Service Ribbon, and Afghanistan Service Ribbon. I'm most proud, though, of having mentored more than 1,000 soldiers.

I plan to continue actively mentoring after I leave military service. Preparing for that time, in every spare moment I'm working on self-improvement and developing the skills I'll need to be a successful entrepreneur.

In addition to the mentors and teachers I mentioned previously, I want to thank my physician, Dr. Dean Miller. He's not only been an amazing doctor, he's also been an amazing friend. When I first told him I planned to transition to male, he said, "I have never had a patient go through this; however, whatever I can do to help you finally become the man you want to become, I will do it." Dr. Miller was the first to support my decision, after my wife and youngest daughter Cierra, and I borrowed and adopted his phrase, "the man you want to become."

I would like to dedicate this chapter to Anibal Ventura, my loving uncle, a man who was like a father to me. He, unfortunately, passed due to COVID-19, but his last words to me were, "I never said this before, but I'm so proud of you. You stuck it out and didn't care what anyone said about you. Don't let anyone hold you back, *ever!*"

Contact Information

Email: Jnicola1976@gmail.com
Facebook: Jayln Nicola
Instagram: Jayln Nicola

Chapter 9

Success Begins
From Within

Christopher King-Hall

We all have the power to be greater than we ever imagined possible, and it all starts within. Living life as the best version of yourself starts with the belief you can accomplish anything upon which you set your mind and focus. Your mindset becomes the focus, and focus becomes energy. Remember, what you focus on and put energy into, good or bad, will manifest in your life.

My goal is to inspire others to be all they can be and to make the world a better place by generating positivity in people's lives with self-courage and self-love. Our energy is a direct outcome of what we share with other people.

The power of mental wealth is within you—it is the power to move our life in any direction. We can choose to be either powerless or the most powerful energy source in our own lives and it all starts with our thought processes.

In this chapter, I share what I believed to be the most powerless time in my life became the most significant and empowering time of my life—a period that would change the trajectory of the rest of my life's journey. My story will give you a glimpse of how I learned, changed, and took control of my health, mindset, belief systems, self-confidence, love, and overall perspective on life. I realized we all can take control of our destiny and shape the life we want to live.

> **You are extraordinary, and it all starts from within.**

I'm reinventing myself by creating the life I want to live through an active lifestyle and my creative passion to inspire people to want to change the world together. There is a humanitarian paradigm shift happening in front of our eyes and we need to take action to shape a better world for our children and those affected by an impoverished, unjust, and unequal racially charged society. There is a burning desire inside of me to help the people I care about and all people who are struggling to live a better life. We are all brilliant-minded people. There is nothing we can't accomplish when we work together to make the world a better place.

A Brief History

It's important for you to know my journey so you can understand my perspectives at a personal level. I've always been a fighter. I don't like to give up. Maybe that was instilled in me when my mother's water broke just 26 weeks into her pregnancy. The doctors warned my parents that my chances of living were slim. Two weeks later, I was born, weighing just two pounds, four ounces. I wanted a shot at life, and I'm still here today because something inside me does not give up, no matter what.

I enjoy life's struggles, and I still look for ways to challenge myself because I know I will grow from each experience. When we have goals and bring purpose and passion into our lives, the inner motivation to defy all odds can make us or break us.

My parents divorced when I was three years old, and their separation launched a childhood filled with changes. As a youth, I often believed my upbringing to be unnecessarily challenging and often wondered how my life would have been different if I had been raised like a "normal person." I laugh at that perspective now, because I've learned to look back on my younger years with a great sense of love and appreciation. The changes I faced gave me an understanding of life that is much richer than if I had lived in the small town of St. Albans, Vermont, for my entire life.

During the next 23 years, I lived in 15 different homes in four states. When I was 27, a good buddy and I drove to the west coast from Vermont, hauling our worldly belongings behind us. Both of us wanted to change our lives drastically, and our heads were filled with "California Dreaming." That's exactly what I got.

One year later, I was living in San Francisco in a five-bedroom house with a dozen Vermont friends, and we all had the desire to create art, music, videos, and chase our dreams.

That was before YouTube, by the way.

Let's backtrack a bit. My burning desire to create and tell stories through visual experiences sprouted while I studied media productions and photography in high school. In college, I studied film production, and after graduation, I went to work at an ABC News affiliate station as an editor and lighting/production grip for the evening news. It was fun, although I soon realized I could make more money doing non-media jobs.

I left ABC and for five years worked at a hospital as a surgical instrument cleaning technician. This work paid well, but it wasn't my true path, didn't feed my purpose, and did not bring me joy. I took a break for a three-month road trip. When I returned, I knew I had to move to California and chase my creative desires there. To prepare and save up for the move, I worked five simultaneous jobs while completing my film certificate program.

Once I moved to the west coast, I quickly settled into California life and eventually became happily married.

I worked in top hotels as their audiovisual (AV) expert, which led me into the live-event AV world. Eventually, I became Director of Event Technologies at a top-tier hotel in the financial district of San Francisco. It was a job I could have had for life and it would have given me a good retirement. However, I didn't feel as though I had purpose. I liked my work yet I knew I still wasn't on my true life path.

The presenters in the events I managed inspired me

when they talked about their visions and world views. There was more to life, and I knew I wanted more. I had always believed I had been born for something greater—something with deeper meaning and purpose.

Changing priorities and passions

Everyone at the hotel appreciated my work ethic; I worked long hours and was committed to always doing an excellent job. But when my first son was born toward the end of 2014, I soon realized I couldn't maintain that work schedule and be the supportive and nurturing father and husband I wanted to be. In February 2015, after five years as director, I gave my notice. It was a difficult decision and I was nervous. I wanted to provide for my family, yet I was determined to make a change. I needed to be home more, and I wanted a freelance lifestyle so I could choose when I wanted to work.

From the beginning of my freelance career, I worked with fifteen clients on a pretty consistent basis, doing live-event AV work, in full control of my schedule. In 2016, almost exactly one year into my new life and just 14 months after our first child was born, we welcomed a second son into the world. It became even more important to give time and support to my family.

After just two years as a freelancer, I was making as much as I had as a director and I was working only two-thirds as many hours. After five years, I was making almost double what I had made as a director, and I became more selective. I chose to work with a handful of companies and had the flexibility to decide what events I wanted to work.

103

Life was busy—I felt in control, yet something was still missing. I was still lacking the purpose I craved. I've always dreamed about being able to change the world some way, somehow—but my actions *weren't* creating or impacting people's lives in a positive way. I *wasn't* changing the world. I still needed to pay the bills, and I needed to be responsible to my family. Could I just walk away from my work and just take time to ponder and create? I didn't think so.

At the beginning of 2020, I was fired up and expecting a record-breaking flurry of events and clients for the year. On the first day of January, I had launched my own media company, Rain Sky Media LLC. I'd named the company after my sons not only to honor them and their importance in my life, but also to serve as a daily reminder of why I need to remain motivated. Using just their middle names gave the three of us a shared secret and a constant source of private happiness. I was working with a brilliant new event space in downtown San Francisco, and its team and I had invested years into creating one of the premier venues in the city.

The year started strong—and came to a halt when the COVID-19 virus hit. Within 72 hours, the majority of the events for the entire year had either been canceled or rescheduled. The lives of everyone around the world changed drastically. Within months, all business was gone, California was in lockdown, and I was home with my family, sheltered in place, focusing on our health as the top priority.

It was a difficult time. I took a deep look inside and asked myself, *How can I use this time to my advantage?*

Where am I in my life and where do I want to go? How can I make this work? I've always looked at adversity as a time to grow and prosper. Now I was about to embark on a new stage in my life, opening up a new state of mind, putting me on the path to change my life forever.

Being a father in my forties made me aware I needed to take care of my health. With thousands of people dying every day, the pandemic raised my awareness to an entirely new level. During the summer of 2020, I began choosing healthier foods, and committed to exercising every day and getting enough sleep. To keep myself paced for success, I set a goal of running a trail marathon and set aside time to run as much as I could. I completed the marathon on my 43rd birthday in the midst of a 100-day stretch of running every day.

After multiple knee surgeries and a rebuilt ACL, I thought my days as a runner were over. Proper nutrition, patience, and persistence changed all that. By the year's end, I'd run 1,241 miles over 263 days. I can't emphasize enough how important healthy choices are for a longer, more prosperous life. Mental wealth comes literally from within, and it starts with what you put into your body.

Don't place limits on what you think you can accomplish. Set your ambitions higher than you think you can achieve. Make sure your goal-setting aligns with your true passions in life. Make sure you have mentors who inspire you and have accountability partners to keep you on track.

With no work in the middle of the pandemic, it would have been easy for me to focus on the bad and complain

105

all of it was unfair—my finances were hurting and my savings were being drained to pay the bills. But it didn't take me long to realize the most important thing to do was to give thanks and be grateful for little things. Perhaps all of the transitions I made in my young life helped me cope better in times of adversity.

Because of the pandemic, I've learned to be more grateful for everything in life. It's true what the leaders and mentors of the world say: *The more you are grateful in life, the more fulfilling a life you will live, the more the universe will give to you, and the more you can prosper and give back to others.*

Okay, we all have bad days! Some are worse than others, that's for sure. There will be days we wish never happened. Just accept the truth: When bad happens, it could always be worse. Also, accept that life puts us through difficult circumstances—not to punish us or to force pain on us—but because the universe needs us to grow and become stronger so we can endure our *true* life purpose.

Gaining mental control of our thoughts is the key to either truly becoming limitless or doing nothing at all. We set our *own* limits by deciding what we can accomplish. You fail the moment you lose faith in yourself or the instant you tell yourself *I can't do this.*

I'm here to tell you this: *Every time you hear doubt in your head, reverse the thought process.* Don't allow yourself to fail because you believe you can't do something. The power is in *you*! Remember that every challenge or failed attempt is just an opportunity to learn and grow. Thomas Edison attempted to perfect the light bulb ten thousand times before he was successful.

You too are a creator without limits, and it all starts from within.

Our mental focus and daily routines can shape our lives to be more fulfilling and prosperous than we ever imagined, while our belief systems can either empower us or hold us back. How many times have you said to yourself *I can't do this!* because you let a bad memory limit you? Don't let the past control your future.

A new perspective

The latest transitional period in my life has opened a gateway for me. In summer 2020, my perspective completely changed when I participated in *Unleash The Power Within,* a virtual Tony Robbins event. Tony introduced me to Master Stephen Co, who introduced me to the art of meditation and the appreciation that we are all beings of divine light and energy. I feel self-reflection and meditation are truly empowering arts, and they help anyone have a great sense of purpose and self-appreciation. I encourage everyone to take time out whenever they can to explore the possibilities in meditation and enrich their life journey.

Every one of us has a purpose in life, a destiny. Now I also see *we have to believe in ourselves.* We have the power to mold our lives to become what we want them to be. Ask yourself what is more painful for you—leaving this life knowing you could have given it more or challenging yourself to give it all you have to give? Start today, take charge, and make a decision that will springboard you in a new direction of your dreams.

I am grateful for every experience in my life, and I truly believe each challenge was a chance to grow. There are no decisions I regret or experiences I didn't deserve. All of my experiences, good and bad, created who I am today. All of the choices we make have consequences, and we must experience them before we're able to fulfill our life's destiny.

Life is a continuous journey and we shouldn't treat it like a destination. Staying hungry and striving for the next goal in life will create a belief system and appreciation for life that can be limitless and continually gratifying.

No matter the odds, *don't give up*. Simply taking responsibility for your expectations and your reactions can absolutely give you power beyond your wildest dreams. Remember, you are extraordinary and it all starts from within. No matter what your talents, you can contribute to the world.

The only difference between being ordinary and extraordinary is your mindset and belief in yourself. Don't ever lose confidence in yourself. Don't let the beliefs of others bring you down or convince you that you are not capable of something great—*especially* if that is something that you're passionate about.

Are you ordinary? No, you are extraordinary!

You are a creator.

Author's Notes

My background is in video production, customer service, and live event audio-visual services; I call myself a visual storyteller.

Born and reared in Vermont, I live in Northern California. I'm a proud husband to Yi, and the father of two young boys, now five and six years old. Being a father and having a loving and supportive wife has

created an immense feeling of love and appreciation in my life. I could not have survived this journey and especially these difficult times without the unwavering love and support of my wife.

Although I've lived a full life, my true journey and purpose in life are just beginning. My chapter is a glimpse into my life story and how the last 12 months have put me on a journey of purpose with a limitless mindset. My goal is to inspire you, so when you believe in yourself and you take action to create your dreams, anything is possible.

Be well, stay amazing, and remember you have the power within! Let's change the world together.

Contact Information

Email: rainskymediallc@gmail.com
Website: http://rainskymedia.com/
Instagram: christopherkinghall

Chapter 10

C-Notes: Currency to Build Your Mental Wealth

Tina Haskins Smith

Wealth is usually associated with finance because it's a game of deposits and withdrawals: The more money you withdraw from your bank account, the less wealthy you become. The more money that builds up in your bank account from your deposits, the wealthier you are.

A parallel theory applies to your mental wealth. The more you build and develop your *confidence, character, competency, connections*, and *community*, the more powerful your mental wealth becomes. I call these five concepts *C-notes*, which is also a term for hundred-dollar bills.

Confidence

With the combination of COVID-19, the economy's downward spiral, and the movement for justice can be overwhelming. Self-doubt can creep into our thinking: *Have I suppressed seeing the injustice that's going on around me? Have I missed speaking up when things were wrong? Have I provided the leadership my teams need since transitioning to a remote workplace?* It's easy to doubt yourself as a leader.

When self-doubts start knocking at my door, I don't let them in. Instead, I let in self-awareness, a far more positive emotion. The two are related, but affect us very differently. Self-doubt can deplete our mental wealth and our confidence. Self-awareness actively builds our confidence.

Confidence, character, competency, connections, and community. . . they are the C-notes—the hundred-dollar bills—that we use to build the balance of our mental wealth.

Self-doubt is a stop sign—a hard stop that paralyzes your mental state. Self-awareness is a yield sign that slows you down while allowing you to continue moving ahead.

We are making withdrawals from our mental wealth if we're consistently paralyzed by self-doubt. We must transition from self-doubt to self-awareness, which allows us to recognize our fears and insecurities as we confidently move ahead to reach our goals.

Character

Emails, meetings, action items, projects . . . I feel the need to respond to everything that comes my way. My perfectionism always rises to the occasion and ensures I complete everything, but I become tired and can border on exhaustion.

We are making withdrawals from our mental wealth when we're always striving for perfection. People wrongly associate perfection with character. I've learned that imperfections build character, and as long as integrity is maintained, imperfection allows us to be more authentic and innovative.

Now I'm learning to pick three things from my never-ending pile to focus on and complete. I know I'm a better leader when I have a sense of accomplishment and I'm not being spread too thin.

One important meeting I will never cancel is the meeting I schedule with myself on a regular basis. I need time to clear my thoughts, spend time with family and friends, contact my doctors for my regular checkups, and exercise.

Competency

I am currently leading the implementation of an electronic healthcare record (EHR) system at the large medical system where I work. This is a sophisticated technology that will make work easier for clinicians providing care and service to our patients and families. I exhibit my competency in processes, project management, and technology while bringing over 10,000

113

people together for a common goal that represents a multi-million-dollar investment.

In the middle of an EHR implementation complicated by a pandemic, decisions are much tougher to make. Using data helps me to make decisions that keep everyone safe, but data alone is not enough. In addition to the facts, when I make my decisions, I use something that can't always be easily explained—and that is wisdom. Over time, we learn we don't have to have all the facts to make a decision. With wisdom, we use a compilation of facts, experience, and discernment to make good decisions. That is a definition of competency.

We are making withdrawals from our store of mental wealth if we think just being smart is enough. Anyone can have book knowledge, but we become mentally stronger when we complement the facts with wisdom. When we exercise discernment along with facts, our competency increases our mental bank account.

Connections

I recently reconnected with a senior executive I'd met at a healthcare industry conference. Our connection could have easily stopped there, but it has extended far beyond our friendship. As a CIO of a major pediatric organization, she knows many people in the medical IT field, and she sends me information about career opportunities. Being introduced to a wide variety of key decision-makers has increased my opportunities for advancement and given me more options. It's great to know her, and I appreciate how she looks out for my interests.

In addition to connecting to decision-makers, I also connect with younger people on their way up through mentoring. I mentor students at Texas A&M University's Mays Business School through AGGIEvisors and also serve as the mentor liaison for the Black and Heritage Network at the Seattle Children's Hospital.

Networking can be challenging for people, especially if you are an introvert. However, it is important to reach beyond our fears and personality to explore new connections. We should also make deposits in other's mental bank accounts by connecting them to people we know.

We are making withdrawals from our mental wealth assets if we think just knowing people is enough. Knowing people who introduce us to others enriches our mental deposits by creating far more options for opportunities and connections. 115

Community

My parents still live in Duncanville, a small suburban city close to both Dallas and Ft. Worth, Texas, where I grew up. It's a friendly community that molded me and invested in me, and it gave me good schools, good opportunities, and good friends. As part of my belief in the community and the future, I invest in STEM initiatives for youths in Duncanville. Healthcare technology is quickly evolving into emerging innovations and careers, and I want to help a new generation find a better path. Literacy is another cause close to my heart that I support.

Giving back to others makes deposits in my mental

bank account. It also humbles me and gives me great hope for the future of our youth, as others did for me.

Now I live and work in Seattle, Washington. As in other major cities, gentrification has occurred and it's hard for lower-income people to find affordable housing and services. The Odessa Brown Children's Clinic, an inner-city facility, is near and dear to my heart; it offers mental health, wellness, and dental services as well as traditional medical programs. I have the honor of giving back to the clinic, not just financially through the Friends of Odessa Brown Children's Clinic Guild, but also through service by partnering with others to provide innovative technology solutions in the new Odessa Brown Children's Clinic.

I've been the recipient of many opportunities that progressed my career; it's important to me that I repay the blessings that came my way and in turn invest in the community in which I live. I'm always looking for organizations or causes to support financially, as well; most of them are in my areas of passion: technology, business, and healthcare. I want to help youth learn more about those fields.

I have been blessed to have two communities, both Duncanville and Seattle, and to be in a position to give back to both. We need to leave a legacy for the next generation. In many ways, serving others enriches our mental wealth and allows us to do even more. Blessings cannot stop with us. They must flow through us to others.

We are making withdrawals from our mental wealth resources if we think just our presence alone is enough

116

of a gift to give to our community. We must invest in the place in which we live. We must leave a legacy in our community reflecting the depth of our mental wealth.

Conclusion

The year 2020 will never be forgotten. It has challenged us in unimaginable ways. In what seemed like an instant, the year stripped us of almost everything we have taken for granted . . . where we eat, what we do for entertainment, how we can gather, our options for learning, where we are allowed to go. Millions have lost their homes and their jobs. Too many have lost their lives.

2020 tested the stability of our mental wealth. All of us have probably had times when we felt mentally overdrawn. Our everyday lives have challenges we never dreamed of. We have established home offices to accommodate working from home. We have become teachers to our children. We have become short-order cooks for our families with snacks and meals around the clock.

However, through it all, we can find ways to build our mental wealth. The pandemic is revealing our imperfections, and each one gives us opportunities to excel. We're developing great character because we are showing we can thrive through tough times.

The stock market has highs and lows. We take for granted that our investments are easily affected by external forces and personal decisions about investments. One day the market is trending up, the next day, the market is heading down, and we're

117

relatively philosophical about it. Most of us keep putting our money in whether it's a bull market or bear market, believing that in the long term, we'll come out far ahead.

Our mental wealth is built the same way our investment wealth in banks and the stock market is built. External forces and personal decisions definitely can affect our mental wealth. However, if we invest more positive deposits into our mental investment account instead of negative withdrawals, we will come out far richer in the long term.

Confidence, character, competency, connections, and community . . . they are the C-notes—the hundred-dollar bills—that we use to build the balance of our mental wealth.

Author's Notes

As a philanthropist and IT executive, I credit my parents, Thomas and Barbara Haskins, for teaching me the importance of work and education along with the value of faith, family, and fun. My experiences in Virginia, Texas, Pennsylvania, New York, Washington, and Spain have contributed to my servant leadership style.

119

Giving to others is a natural part of my life, and I support a wide variety of organizations, including Black Girls CODE, Dignity for Divas, Metropolitan Seattle Sickle Cell Task Force, The Links, Beacon Hill Preparatory Institute, Housing Solutions for Hope Guild, Friends of Odessa Brown Children's Clinic Guild, and Seattle Children's Research Institute. I'm a proud member of Delta Sigma Theta, Incorporated, and served on the board of Texas HOPE Literacy, Inc., when I lived in Texas.

My degrees are a B.B.A. in Business Analysis (Management Information Systems) from Texas A&M University, and an M.B.A. in Management from Amberton University. My additional specialized training includes the CHIME Healthcare CIO Boot Camp and Harvard School of Public Health–Leadership Strategies for Information Technology in Health Care.

Past positions have included stints as Assistant Vice President, Program Management Office Director, and ITIL Service Delivery Manager with a Project Management Professional Certification and ITIL v3 Foundation Certification. I've worked in a variety of industries and organizations, including American Airlines, IBM, First American/Transamerica Real Estate Tax Service, Parkland Health & Hospital System, and Cook Children's Health Care System.

Now a Seattle resident, I'm the Senior IT Director of Enterprise Clinical Systems and Epic Project Director at Seattle Children's Hospital. I start my days with devotional time and a workout, and listen to podcasts and read books to continue to learn and grow. I love hanging out with my sister and my long-term friends, and dote on my nephews and nieces, receiving the "Aunt of the Year" award from them every year.

While 2020 saw unprecedented darkness and trouble, I look forward to a lifetime of service, happiness, and mental wealth.

Contact Information:

Email: Tina.Haskins.Smith@gmail.com
LinkedIn: www.linkedin.com/in/TinaHaskinsSmith

Chapter 11

Build Your Mental Wealth With Joy, Not Jealousy

Joe Peach Graves

D id you know that the hardest mountain to climb isn't the tallest? It isn't the steepest, the most jagged, or the most slippery. It has nothing to do with hazards or weather. The hardest mountain to climb is the one you didn't see coming until you slam into it. It's also the one you aren't equipped or prepared to climb.

Think of a time in your life when you had the rug pulled out from under you, and the last thing you wanted to hear was why you should look on the bright side.

When I stood 19,341 feet above Tanzania at the peak of Mt. Kilimanjaro, I had no idea that my greatest challenge was still waiting for me. A week later, after spending time on safari with one of my closest friends and mentors, I was on my way home from Africa and looked forward to seeing my wife and daughter. I was still exhilarated and thrilled by having climbed the world's largest free-standing mountain, something beyond the wildest dreams of most people. Ready to get on the plane, standing alone in the Addis Ababa Bole International airport, I read a Facebook message: Divorce papers were ready for me to sign and I should pick my daughter up from my wife's boyfriend's house once I landed.

I felt gutted.

You can reach a new level of mental strength and health when you don't waste your energy on jealousy, pain, and unhappiness.

Right now you probably have questions, and the big one is *What's in this chapter to help me?*

Maybe you have experienced the pain of seeing a relationship come to an end. Maybe you learned that someone whom you love is in love with someone else. Maybe none of this relates to you, but you're just curious. What *I* know is this: the relationships we build reflect the most important aspects of our lives. If you want to grow your mental wealth in the realm of relationships, you might be able to learn a thing or two.

Just before I wrote this chapter, our family celebrated my daughter Jolinda's eighth birthday, which she happily said it was the best day ever. Most people can't imagine how my family got where we are now from where we were the day I was walloped with an unexpected divorce. It may seem even more improbable to realize I work with families all over the world and help them learn a mindset of *compersion,* the first step on the path to living in Paradise Forever.

Love really does conquer all. Loving intentionally is how I survive and thrive after my rather traumatic forced change. I believe most people want to love unconditionally, and they do manage to do so until conditions occur that they're not prepared for. What brings me joy is helping people prepare mentally to love in *all* conditions, so they can focus on shining their light in the universe. I am passionate about this mission beyond all things, other than the love I have for my daughter.

123

Compersion is the opposite of jealousy. It's an ability that exists in all of us—the ability to feel joy in others' happiness. When I worked at Walt Disney World, I saw this emotion all the time. I witnessed a lot of it, performing with my friend Goofy, who I've known for years. Imagine the world before COVID-19, when after waiting in line for hours, a child finally has a turn to give Goofy the biggest hug ever.

The joy the child and his family feel is completely understandable. What I found even more amazing is the joy shared by people just walking past when they catch a glimpse of the child's ecstatic hug—they smile, melt a little, and share in the love. There is a strong possibility you at this very moment are smiling at the vision of a little kid getting blissed out with Goofy love.

Think about it. You're not feeling the joy and love because it's you or your child hugging Goofy. You're not feeling jealous because the anonymous child got a hug from Goofy instead of your child (or you!).

The joy you feel is *compersion*. It's such a beautiful concept, but most people have never heard the word. In fact, your phone or computer will try to correct your spelling if you type it as a text or in a letter, but that is how it's spelled.

Compersion is not used widely because it's primarily associated with polyamorous relationships. Its definitions include the love and joy one feels for their partner when they are doing *much* more than just hugging Goofy.

At Disney, we shared a joke about Mickey Mouse going to relationship counseling with Minnie Mouse. Mickey shares why he is having a problem. The counselor says, surprised, "Mickey, be reasonable. You know Minnie is a cartoon character. Why are you so upset that she's a little silly?"

Mickey snaps, "I didn't say she was a little silly. I said she was f****ing Goofy."

The day I auditioned and earned a role as a Disney cast member, I heard this joke for the first time. Little did I know then that I would get married and have an ethically non-monogamous relationship with the mother of my child, a woman I love and respect to this day.

I know what you're thinking: *How can you believe in compersion if you lost your wife?*

But, you see, my divorce actually solidified my belief in compersion. I recognize how well this mindset has served me in our relationship, in business, and life as a whole, ever since I got the news when I was alone in Ethiopia.

Climbing Kilimanjaro and going on safari was part of the most epic vacation of my life. It was a vacation I earned partly through the joy I receive in helping others have joy. As a professional tourist, I work to help improve the quality of people's lives by showing them how wonderful vacationing feels and providing them with access to systems designed to save them money— and even make money—by living their best life.

The more people I help, the more money and opportunity for travel I earn. Because of this work and my genuine love for seeing the world, I've been to 43 countries and 38 states in the United States. I genuinely want to see the joy on my family's and friends' faces, so it came pretty easy to me and I excelled from the beginning. 125

Before I left on this vacation, I spent a few weeks visiting family in Colorado and California, before heading northwest to spend my birthday with my mother. She lives in a beautiful little house on the Oregon coast in a town that's so small, if I said its name, people would know the house. The two of us spent a couple of days alone, then my wife and daughter flew in from Honolulu to help me celebrate. We ate breakfast at the Pig & Pancake and had an amazing day playing in my mom's yard with her dog.

After Jolinda went to sleep, my wife and I went out for a night on the town. We shared what I still remember as one of the best days of my life. The next day my wife flew off to attend one of our company conventions, and I went to Africa. I wasn't aware that was the last night we'd spend together as a married couple.

While I was in Africa, though my wife was surrounded by our team members and friends, she says she felt alone. For the last year, she'd been dating a guy off and on, and he didn't share our belief in compersion. She decided she didn't believe in it anymore, either, after our ten years together, and she was ready for a monogamous relationship. She picked up Jolinda at my mom's house, went back to Hawaii, and reconnected with the man who is now her husband.

I honestly believe he is a really great guy, and appreciate the amazing opportunities he has given my (now) ex-wife and daughter. Don't get it wrong. Despite my belief in compersion, divorce was not remotely fun; it is very painful. I was aware of him as her boyfriend the whole time, and I knew he loved her, yet I had absolutely *no* expectations our marriage would end. We had a life together, a child, a business, and I believe, a shared deep love. Now I was suddenly faced with crippling debt, custody issues, and the loss of a nearly 10-year partnership, in business as well as in marriage.

Again, I know what you're thinking: *You aren't really selling this whole compersion idea. It sounds terrible.*

Okay, I have a question for you: *What if I hadn't known about the guy at all?* Studies suggest one in three unmarried and one in five married relationships experience some form of infidelity. Think about it. You may have had an extramarital fling, or surely you know someone else who has been on one side or another of an affair.

One of the main differences in a compersion-based relationship is there's *honesty* between partners rather than lying.

Another advantage of a compersion-based relationship is it's an amazing feeling when you are comfortable sharing everything with your partner. The freedom to speak about and act on the things you really want without guilt or judgment is more fulfilling than most will ever understand. The incredible sex, financial abundance, adventure, love, joy, passion (and did I say incredible sex?), that I've had through my belief in the power of compersion has been life-changing. I'll share more in my next book.

I don't plan to become polyamorous, so why even read this chapter, you wonder.

So, how *can* compersion help you? You don't need to change your monogamous lifestyle. Compersion is a philosophy that doesn't need to include any sexual extremes. It can simply be your conscious choice to reduce jealousy. It's a sign of mental strength.

I have an exercise for you. On a sheet of paper, draw a big plus sign, creating four quadrants on the page. On one line write *Joy* and on the line that crosses it write *Pain.* All the relationships you will ever have can be described on this sheet of paper. There will be moments in each quadrant in almost every relationship, but there will usually be a focus on one.

Schadenfreude. This German word describes the joy you feel when someone feels unhappiness, misfortune, or pain. (This is pronounced *shah*-duhn-

froy-duh, and literally translates as *harm-joy*.) If you are in a relationship like this, your partner had better remember their safe word.

All jokes aside, very few people will admit to living in this quadrant, but they are out there. Actually, almost all of us feel schadenfreude sometimes. With our current political climate, regardless of what side you are on, there will be a lot of people who will feel joy when the other side loses. My mentor and co-author Johnny Wimbrey calls them *wolves*. They actually experience joy as they exercise their purpose to kill, steal, and destroy.

Jealousy. The next quadrant is for those of us who feel pain when someone feels joy—the *opposite* of compersion. Beyond feeling awful, living in this quadrant can create major problems. Have you ever had a friend snag a position or a customer that you wanted? How did it make you feel and did that feeling serve you?

Competition can be a motivator, but my belief is that friendly competition is better than a bitter rivalry. I teach my daughter to be a good winner and a better loser. When she doesn't win, she says with a smile, "Great job, I'm going to beat you next time!" This is a mantra in our family that helps us maintains drive without succumbing to jealousy.

Empathy. The third quadrant is when you feel pain at the pain of others. Too many people live in the empathy quadrant, simply because they don't want to live in the first two and they don't understand the last one. While being empathetic may seem like good, generous quality, many don't take any action to find their way out of pain. They wallow in the pain and end up just attracting more pain. Remember, the first and best step to eradicating poverty is to not be in poverty yourself. In much the same way, the best way to eradicate sadness is to not be sad.

Compersion. If you really think about it, this is the square that everyone should want to live in. Right? It's where the party's at, but more importantly, it is where the mentally strong, mentally healthy folks live.

This concept is what helped me climb Kilimanjaro. When my business partner and former cruise director, Ray Carr, asked me to join him on this adventure, I had never even considered climbing any mountain. I worked with my father on his site, *AfricanJewelry.com*, so I knew I'd go to Africa someday, but hadn't thought of Tanzania. I owned no climbing gear, and because I 129 live on Oahu, I can't stand the cold. I'm a wimp and firmly believe schools should close at anything below 60 degrees. The only reason I agreed to go is that I wanted to see Ray make it to the top, and I knew my being there would help him make the ascent. As I took step after step up that mountain, somehow freezing and sweating at the same time, my determination to get him to the top kept me going.

The ascent was thrilling, and I am glad for every moment of our trek. We camped at just over 15,000 feet the night before we reached the summit, and I saw an unforgettable, otherworldly scene that will inspire me for my whole life. We were above the clouds that night, and it was so cold that frost settled on top of the fluffy white clouds hugging the mountain below us. The stars reflected off the frost, twinkling below me, and I felt as though I was drifting in outer space.

If I hadn't been focused on serving the joy of others, I never would have the opportunity to be there for that rare sight.

They say luck is what happens when preparation meets opportunity. Compersion is the mindset that prepared me for the greatest challenges and the greatest accomplishments in my life. I truly feel it has enriched my mind.

When Jolinda turned eight years old, she was surrounded by the love, support, and cooperation of both her parents, her stepfather, my partner and her son, one of my lovers along with her girlfriend and her girlfriend's boyfriend, who just happens to be my cousin and lives with us. It is the family we choose. I could have allowed jealousy to rob my daughter of that experience.

How much has jealousy cost you?

You can reach a new level of mental strength and health when you don't waste your energy on jealousy, pain, and unhappiness. I invite you to stop living in a quadrant of pain. Choose *joy*—live your life with compersion.

130

Author's Notes

As the great-great-grandchild of a runaway slave, I was raised in the spirit of generational improvement. I'm known both as a jack of all trades and a visionary leader, and my varied career paths and life experiences have given me some unique insights and the ability to connect with just about anyone. Being reared in Hawaii and having the pleasure of traveling to more than 40 countries and nearly every state has given me a perspective on paradise, plus the means to find happiness and freedom.

The majority of my entertainment career was spent with the Walt Disney Company, where an understanding of the Happiest Place on Earth expanded my mindset to the point that I learned anything is possible. When I was an assistant cruise director on the Norwegian Cruise Lines flagship, I gained an understanding of leading teams and exceeding expectations. My experience as an athlete and as a champion gamer honed my competitive nature. I also participate in slam poetry contests.

My experience as a father created my demand for a brighter future plus the patience and passion to teach. A combination of these and other life experiences gives me the ability to inspire and educate learners to find solutions toward increase. With the belief that success is the progressive realization of a worthy ideal, I guide students on a path of self-discovery. Living in paradise forever is a reality every human can achieve, beginning right now.

I live in my own Hawaiian paradise, sharing custody of my daughter, Jolinda Peach Kamana'olana Graves, and increasing my love daily.

Contact Information:

Email: joepeach@paradiseforeverhawaii.com
Facebook: Joseph Peach Graves
Instagram: @paradiseforeverhawaii

Chapter 12

You're Gonna Make It After All

Toni L. Pennington

I'm gonna write through it, cry through it,
live through it, love through it,
pray through it,
be blue through it,
but I'm going to get through it.

Research and experience tell me mental health directly correlates with mental wealth. The *Oxford English Dictionary* (OED) defines health as, "Soundness of body; that condition in which its functions are duly and efficiently discharged." The OED defines wealth as, "The condition of being happy and prosperous; well-being." Combined, the two suggest that being mentally and emotionally healthy, and making sure you are in a good place with both, will produce a wealth of body, mind, soul, and spirit.

I'm not a psychologist, but it sure makes sense to me. That good place—that sweet spot—sounds like the place we'd all like to be.

We're going through a dark time in our history, and it makes that sweet spot more difficult to visualize and attain. It's important that we try, however, for the work we do right now will make us better, healthier, and stronger for an uncertain future.

2020 was an extremely difficult year for every human being on earth. At the time of this writing, we are all learning what it means to show love from an acceptable social distance, what it means to cook every meal at home, *Most of us don't realize the depth of our mental wealth until we face astounding situations.* and, for many of us, what it means to reconnect with our families. The coronavirus pandemic has taught us how to live alone together (no, that is not an oxymoron). It has also given us an opportunity to spend time with ourselves, our thoughts, and our deepest feelings. We have the rare opportunity to be silent and reflective.

I had no idea this would be one of the most painful times in my life.

I have written about surviving traumatic situations before, but never while I was in the midst of one. As I

134

write this chapter, I have just suffered a devastating loss. The unimaginable happened—the love of my life died suddenly.

In my previous writings, I didn't share his name because people aren't always glad for you when you're happy. They don't always root for you, unfortunately. We were very private about our relationship, and that allowed us to nurture it and give it what it needed without prying eyes or opinions. Within our bubble, we added to each other's lives. The decision to maintain our privacy allowed our collective mental wealth to grow and strengthen. We healed and made each other better; those details are for a different story. One day, perhaps.

My love was the world-renowned, Grammy-award-winning drummer and percussionist Jeff "LO" Davis. He was known as the Godfather of Gospel Drumming. In his nearly four-decade career, he appeared on over 300 albums and worked in almost every musical genre. Jeff played with everyone from Richard Smallwood to Sting to Stevie Wonder.

While he wasn't a household name, among his peers, colleagues, and those he tutored and mentored, Jeff was a highly respected, polished, professional musician with his own distinct sound. He was a teacher and lover of music and an even greater lover of God and the gospel of Jesus Christ. He was a good man who always had ministry on his mind, whether it was feeding the homeless, making their lives better, or teaching young musicians how they should behave and carry themselves in church as well as in the music industry.

On many occasions, I watched musicians of every age hang onto Jeff's every word and motion as he conducted clinics. They knew he had seen it all. Jeff generously shared his mental wealth, pouring out everything he had, praying that what he offered would enhance the lives of those around him. To my amazement, Jeff didn't realize how beloved and unique he was. On the drive home, he would be shocked as I shared what I witnessed: Everyone in the room had been on the edge of their seats, taking in his every word. His humility was overwhelming. We were only granted six short years together, but they were rich years. I am brokenhearted but still grateful.

The desire to share knowledge is something we had in common. As a tutor, I take great pleasure in giving what I have if it helps the student reach their goal. I understand why sharing is called "the gift of giving." There is a profound feeling of fulfillment when you give someone else what they need. When you give freely, you change lives. Sometimes you will never know who you've reached; people may appear years later and let you know how a small thing you did or said changed their life. If that's not powerful, I don't know what is!

My brother says there is a nugget of selfishness in sharing: While you accomplish a good deed, you in turn feel good about yourself. I agree, but it's more complex than just stroking your ego. Externally, it appears that you are giving something; doing a good deed, but internally you experience a change. That change fortifies you. It enhances your sense of kindness, caring, and empathy. That practice helps stock your mental wealth treasure chest. It helps free you from the guilt of selfishness and puts what is good in your life into perspective. You probably know the saying,

"I cried when I had no shoes,
then I met a man with no feet"
—**Mahatma Gandhi**

Being able to share what you've learned is the ultimate mental wealth. When you are a giving person, rich in kindness and love, it is my experience that the same comes back to you exponentially.

There is a caveat: You should always give from your heart, never with the expectancy of a reward. Give graciously with an unexpectant heart and allow the blessings to fall upon you when it's time. That time will most likely be when you need something the most.

You may be asking, what was the point of telling you of my loss? Well, what I needed for my mental wealth changed. When Jeff died, I was finishing a graduate school class, in the midst of trying to push through my final project, and I was struggling. Ironically, I was working on two papers, one entitled "What Does Loss Feel Like", and the other, "I Don't Remember Crying." Talk about foreshadowing.

Universities don't have generous bereavement policies for their students, so I was forced to focus and push through my grief as I researched and wrote my papers. I knew how proud Jeff was of my work, and that was instrumental in my getting the job done. He always told me he admired me and I inspired him every day

137

with my work ethic as it related to my studies and my students. I didn't realize he was silently watching me, and Jeff didn't know his words replenished me; they meant so much because I admired and respected him. Yes, we had a low-key, mutual admiration society. I kept his words, gestures, and memories stored in my mental health chest, where they sustained me and my mental wealth as I grieved.

That leads me to the concept of knowing what you need. As a writer, you can become detached from the subject matter, paying closer attention to the process, making sure your writing makes sense, flows well, and is understandable. You just look at the words objectively. I became so engrossed in the work I didn't notice how personal the stories were and where they were headed.

138

Each story unwrapped a time of profound crisis in my life, a calamity during which I had to find mental wealth, a way to survive. The loss of my mother at a very young age and my own devastating, life-changing health issues were the basis of the stories. I had no intention of going so deeply into past pain and healing, but it was clear I needed this catharsis because once again my life changed. This new tragedy was even more surreal, and all of this was happening as the whole world shifted course and was learning to navigate a plague.

To maintain my mental wealth and health, I deliberately faced my own feelings.

Logically, I knew it would do me no good to try to act like everything was the same because it wasn't. I had to accept my life had changed and I had to change with it.

I made a decision to feed my mind with positive things, happy memories, and pleasant thoughts. I had a lot to draw from in the midst of my sadness, and it was stored in my mental wealth treasure chest. I used the necessary amounts to get through the end of that class. I used a little more to get through the next one. Intuitively, I realized I needed to always keep something on reserve.

Don't get me wrong. I wasn't skipping around the house acting like everything was great. I cried when I needed to cry. I still do. I stopped when I needed to stop, and I felt the heartache when something as simple as someone clapping the same way he did would remind me that I could only hear him in my dreams. There was no getting around that. But exercising my right (and filling my need) to feel a full range of emotions contributed to my mental wealth, my stockpile of wealth builders, which I am happy to share.

Know what you need. This can be a little tricky because initially, you may not know what that is. Sometimes we don't realize what works for us until a situation is forced upon us. For example, you may need to get out and get some fresh air. You've been perfectly happy inside, but after you go outdoors, let a breeze brush your face or hear the birds sing, you may realize how restorative a change of scenery can be.

Another example is good old-fashioned laughter. That one really works for me. When I was diagnosed with HIV, I was afraid that I would never laugh again. On my way home from that appointment, I saw something really funny and burst into a long, loud crack-up in my

139

car. I was grateful because I felt as though God, at that moment, heard my plea for some sense of normalcy, and He answered immediately. It felt like a miracle. These things contribute to your mental wealth and well-being.

Know when you need to talk. Generally, we can feel when we need to speak to someone. We might need a therapist or just a sympathetic ear, someone who knows you and is aware of what you are going through. Perhaps it might be someone who doesn't know what's happening with you, but you trust and rely on their wisdom and sensitivity. Use your judgment.

Know when you need silence. When word was getting out that my love had died, I was sitting at home alone. My brother and several of my sister-friends immediately wanted to come to my aid. "We won't say anything if you don't want, we'll just be there." The cities and states were just beginning to lock down so my sister couldn't get to me.

Thank God for love. I was so appreciative of their offers, but my heartache was so big that there was no room in my home for anyone or anything but me and my pain. I knew that another human being in my space would just annoy me, even if they didn't say a word. I truly needed to be alone and mourn in silence. I didn't have the capacity to worry about anyone else's feelings if I burst into tears if I wanted to roll around on the floor and scream, if I wanted to cut off all my hair (I wasn't going quite that far), but I was sure I needed to be by myself.

Know when you need space and when you need company. Two days into my grief, I asked my brother if he would come over. He did. When he was ready to leave, I didn't want him to go. I had switched from wanting to be alone to needing the comfort of his presence. I realized each situation gave me strength and security because the timing had been right.

When I was alone, I was wrapped in Jeff's love, and there was no room for anyone else in my space. That would have been an intrusion. That time was only meant for Jeff and me. When my brother came, he knew I was trying to be strong. When he hugged me, I turned into a bag of water and let out the tears I didn't know I had been holding. Then we sat silently until I cried again. I did not know what I needed. Thank God others did.

What happens when you're not sure what you need? What works for me is being still and giving my spirit the chance to tell me. It's finding ways to feed my mind and my heart.

Building mental wealth isn't much different than accumulating financial wealth. You've got to figure out what it will take for you to survive (or thrive) in much the same way you calculate the income you need to live comfortably. To do this right, you must take some private time and sit, perhaps meditate, and ask yourself the hard questions. No one else will listen in, so you can tell yourself the pure, unadulterated truth. Then write it down and hide it in a safe place where your thoughts cannot be compromised.

Most of us don't realize the depth of our mental wealth until we face astounding situations. When we look back, we're amazed at the way we handled them. I challenge you to look over your life and find at least

141

one experience where you didn't think you would make it but you did.

That is your triumph—your treasure chest of mental wealth.

Author's Notes

Though I've been a singer since my childhood, my creative energy is now focused on my writing. I've been published many times in PATHS, a literary publication of New Jersey City University. In 2018, I co-authored *Break Through* featuring Toni L. Pennington with Les Brown and several international authors.  More recently, I co-authored *P.U.S.H.: Persist Until Success Happens,* with Matt Morris, Johnny Wimbrey, Sashin Govender, and other well-known authors. My books are found on my own website, listed below, and on Amazon.

143

I hold a Bachelor of Arts degree in English from New Jersey City University, where I work as an academic success coach and tutor mentor, and I'm completing a Master of Arts degree at Southern New Hampshire University. I was born in Brooklyn, New York, and now live in Jersey City, New Jersey.

Contact Information

Email: joyforeverenterprises@gmail.com
Website: joyforeverenterprises.com
Instagram: @Joyforever1love

Chapter 13

Consciousness, the Holy Grail of Mental Wealth

Jiri Urbanek

It is much better to have control over our lives and actions than to be a victim, letting ourselves be swept away by whatever circumstances happen to us. Adapting the practice of consciousness, a simple but powerful behavior makes everyone's life better.

Consciousness—being awake and aware of my surroundings—helped me to overcome the toughest times in my life. I know it can certainly help you, too.

Even though we don't like to admit it, our subconscious minds are programmed by what affects us from outside. During any crisis (and it doesn't matter if it's a personal one or a worldwide pandemic), we keep hearing a drumbeat of fear and disaster: Everything is going wrong, nothing is going right. Our minds follow those drums right down the path of despair, making the situation even worse than it is.

When that happens, it is the right time to increase consciousness using common sense: *Challenge the status quo.* Ask questions and start to think rationally. Avoid being manipulated by emotions, wrong models, prejudice, and manipulations, both your own and those created by others.

> **Consciousness, gratefulness, hope, and optimism are the hallmarks of those who are open to change, welcome responsibility, and use all possibilities that they actively discover.**

146

Realize the power of emotion and learn to not succumb to it; instead, use it for your own benefit. That is what it's all about.

I'll give you an example. When I was diagnosed with multiple sclerosis in 2009, an incurable neurological disease that may lead to full disability, I fell into a very deep depression. I was paralyzed by fear. Rhetorical, stupid questions popped up in my mind every day: *Why me? What caused it?* I searched for information about the disease on the internet, called friends who were doctors, and read everything I could.

Despite my own medical education and knowledge, I did not find any information anywhere that gave me reason to hope. I was only able to create negative scripts in my mind, thinking about the day when I would stop walking and spend the rest of my life lying on my bed. As my life became more and more desperate, I envisioned every possible bad outcome from the disease. Though I received the best treatment, I did not expect any improvement because I was ready to be disabled in the future.

That is the power of negative thinking.

Even worse, I started to transfer my negativity to others. I was mean to people around me, even my children. I saw myself as a victim without control over my life, and what's even sadder, I started to like it. If there was something, I did not want to do, or I screwed up, I always had an excuse: "What do you want from me? I am seriously ill."

One day I realized I could not live my life that way. I had already lost my independence and freedom to my fear and illness, and even my ability to make good decisions was fast being eroded. Living like that was devastating me and the people around me, those whom I loved the most. I started to increase my consciousness and think rationally. I evaluated my condition objectively, from the outside, as I would for someone else. Without fear or negativity—without emotions.

I began to see the positive aspects. I became grateful that I could still walk and do almost everything I did before, just with minor limitations. I changed my mindset from victim to creator, bit by bit.

As I set a goal to live a full, high-quality life, I made a plan. Positivity, gratefulness, and hope were the first steps, then I began to change my bad habits and eliminate the aggravators of my disease. I accepted the

147

fact that my disease was a consequence of my earlier bad decisions. This was not about being sorry about what happened, but about conscious analysis of causes. Health is closely connected with the mental setup and attitude to life. And I consciously helped my doctors by maintaining an active, optimistic attitude and the desire to regain my lost health.

This was not easy, but good things don't come the easy way. It took me three years of my life to make these changes. Consciousness helped me to gain my life back. Today, I live my life at 100% of my health and capacity. I'm happy, satisfied, and I can do anything without limitations.

That episode of my life clearly showed me we attract whatever we feel and believe. If you are focused on bad things, bad things happen. Such is the power of our consciousness, whether spoken or thought. It is up to us whether it unfolds in a good or a bad direction.

Believe it or not, you can influence the way a situation unfolds with your positive mindset.

But it is tricky. Our subconscious always tries to pull us back, back to our "easy" life, actions, and habits— even if they are bad for us. If you let your subconscious win, you will never succeed.

Our habits, actions, and behavioral traditions are very resistant to change. Once you aren't one of the sheep in a herd any longer, people start to think that something is wrong with you. They don't accept your freedom to choose your way. They try to pull you back, blaming you, even attacking you, simply because they want you to be like them. Often, they use emotional pressure.

A surprising number of people live their lives within the artificial boundaries they've defined for themselves. How many times did you want something but held back? I am sure you found some rational explanation why it was impossible—*It's too difficult . . . it would be selfish*—or the immortal phrase *I'll do it later.*

When you're on your deathbed, all those self-imposed restrictions will cause you to say *I did not live the life I wanted.* Why? It's because we erect barriers to keep us from taking advantage of the possibilities.

When you ask people why they remain in conditions that suck, you'll hear, *It cannot be changed; I have had this all my life; I cannot do it; or What would people say*. What nonsense! It's just their indolence and a false sense of security. What they're really saying is, *It sucks but I am in control*. The stereotypes we create simplify ¹⁴⁹ the processing of information and automate mental processes. We're not aware because stereotypical reactions are automatic and subconscious.

Consciousness opens your eyes to see a different world. It is really hard to resist your subconscious, but you can choose to reject an emotionally conditioned request or extortion. You have the right to make your own choices at any given moment. The other party's reaction to the decision is *their* choice. Do they choose to be sad, offended, irritated, silent, or to rejoice and be happy? Their reaction is *not* your business, not ever! ***We are only responsible for our own feelings! Period, full stop.***

Our emotions do shake us up from time to time despite ourselves, and then we ask *what did we do wrong? How can we make it right again?* This is a higher level of consciousness.

Our conscious and subconscious selves are hardwired inside our brains. The part of our brains called neocortex is responsible for rational decisions, analytical behavior, and speech. The more primitive part of the brain, the limbic, is responsible for emotions such as trust, loyalty, behavior, decisions, and reinforcing behavior. The limbic does not control speech, so it can't speak up rationally and join the conversation with the neocortex.

If we manage to communicate with the limbic system using emotional communication, we hit the decision-making spot directly. That is why we prefer to accept emotional messages rather than using analytical thinking, and that's what hurts us in critical situations.

150   It's very important to control our thinking. How many times a day do you catch yourself thinking of something other than you intended to? Too often it's negative thoughts, re-evaluating something that happened in the past that affected our performance poorly. Even though we know that we can't change or control the past, our minds easily get trapped into thinking about our mistakes and failures.

Don't we agree in theory that if we cannot control or change something, we should never let it distract us? We can clearly see this distraction affecting athletes in particular. Rather than concentrating on their performance, they have all sorts of negative thoughts running through their mind, *especially* the times they performed badly in the past—and so their current performance is doomed.

It's daily work to improve and strengthen our consciousness. One of the most important actions we can take is to make an appointment with ourselves. This quiet time with ourselves is insightful, helping us to sort out our thoughts and make sure we're going in the right direction. We get strength to fulfill our resolutions and to define other, better resolutions and goals. We should find room for improvement and progress.

It's not that complicated. Reach for an interesting book, meditate, calm down, and think of yourself. The best way for me is to relax and think is while cruising in my 1968 Buick.

Perhaps you're afraid of what problems you'll find when you are alone with yourself, in peace and quiet? Don't worry, the realization that something is amiss is the beginning of the conversion to becoming a creator. 151 *Before any progress, there must be acknowledgment there's dissatisfaction with the current state of affairs.*

I perform this exercise often and it always leads me to new decisions. It's about finding a good balance between emotions and rational thinking.

We have to survive in our environment—in our community, family, school, work—so we can't do whatever we want. Well, we *can*, but we then have to accept the consequences. In any case, we can set acceptable boundaries and create our unique vision of freedom and success. It is in our hands.

My plan for change always starts with defining *why* I want to make this change. With more age and experience, my vision of my life's purpose is shifting away from just my own paycheck and well-being to helping others and seeing the wider picture. Yes, money is important, yet consciousness helps us develop a desire for fulfillment, doing something to help people around us, something of real value.

This happened to me a few years ago. I was a successful manager in a pharmaceutical company, thinking I was living the white-collar, upper-middle-class life. Instead, I was actually living in a golden cage. For many years, I believed the pharma industry helps people to get better treatment, so I convinced myself I was really helping people. As I became more involved in the inner workings of the business, I learned it doesn't have much to do with helping people. Pharma is purely a money-making business, fighting for market share and profit while being wrapped in a façade of helping people.

I trained people on how to present pharmaceutical products, how to communicate, even how to balance on the fine edge between promotion and manipulation. I developed a method called *Emotional Selling*. The positive effect on sales and profit was enormous in every European country where I implemented it. But there was a little problem: Emotional Selling does not follow pharma industry myths, rigid rules, and old habits. It's more about finding self-confidence and people's positive mindset. It is more about finding a common need and solution than about a simple victory over someone. In sum, it's about how to avoid being manipulated.

This was my first step in the direction of helping others. I realized "normal" people need such training more than salespeople and managers. So, I created emotional selling for "normal people," and described the process in a book I wrote with a provocative title: *I Take No Sh*t*. (By the way, it's only available in Czech; the English version is still in the works.)

I found my *why*—my purpose in life—and it's to help others. That is good, but how do I manage it? On one side, I found my passion; on the other hand, I had bills to pay.

So, like most people in similar situations, I made the wrong decision. I kept my job and my financial stability, and I postponed escaping my golden cage.

I know now that if there is something in your life that you don't like, you must change it quickly. Consciously find the time to look for opportunities and do not be afraid of changes. Expect some effort, hard work, and discomfort, even criticism, and displeasure from others. If, however, your goal is motivated by your heart and desire and based on common sense, you will succeed—*and you will be happy.*

I stayed in my golden cage and lived my unsatisfactory life until 2019. That was the toughest year of my life. Really.

On January 2, 2019, my father suddenly died. On the same day, a postman brought me a foreclosure notice for our house, a result of the debts my father left, and I was given two weeks to put together $9,000 to avoid default. In March, I was fired from my job with the pharma company. Later that year, my mother attempted suicide and ended up in a psychiatric hospital for four months, and I traveled 200 miles twice a week to visit her. In May, my partner Lucie went on a six-month sick leave,

153

which was followed by her losing her pharma industry job, too.

A tough year, right? Yet I survived all this because I was able to consciously manage every problem, solving one issue after another, setting clear goals and solutions. That does not mean that the crises didn't affect my emotions; emotions are always there. Anger, sadness, excitement, desperation . . . everything you can imagine. It is really easy to succumb to the negative and blame the world, God, or whomever, and sit in a corner and cry, but those are the actions of a victim.

Do not blame the world around you for your miserable life, do not pity yourself, and do not complain. That's how victims behave. A creator, on the other hand, decides what will happen.

154
Living through sad moments does not prevent us from having an optimistic view of life; just live through the situation and put it aside. Even a bad situation brings something good. It was meant to teach us something, but we learn and then don't need it anymore. Realization and learning are positive things. *Be positive.*

Here are the lessons I learned:

Consciousness, gratefulness, hope, and optimism are the hallmarks of those who are open to change, welcome responsibility, and use all possibilities that they actively discover. Let us be grateful for what we have even though we ask for more. Gratitude and appreciation are signs of maturity. Consciousness helps you manage all the situations life brings. Consciousness helps you find solutions and make plans, and it keeps you focused on problem-solving.

Everything was turned upside—in a very positive way—in 2019. The drastic changes and the problems I solved strengthened my trust in consciousness and its importance. It also sorted the people around me. It really showed who I can rely on to stand by my side during the hard times, my real friends. I am grateful for these people around me, especially my partner, Lucie. She helped me so, so much.

When my life changed in 2019, I was 47 years old. Now I fully enjoy my freelance existence. I have a chance to really help people, and not only in my private life. I finished my MBA and found a passion for network marketing. I love it. I love the equity of the MLM system, love the real cooperation, and the ability to help others to succeed.

Be aware, determination of success is only in our heads. Believe it or not, we can *attract* success by conscious positive thinking, confidence, and a positive mindset. In other words, everyone has the capacity to achieve whatever they want.

How do we do it? Emotions are manageable, and I have already demonstrated that by controlling them we increase our potential for success. Our limits are only in our minds. Once we admit this, we can start pushing the limits. *Consciously!*

Author's Notes

My training as a veterinarian led me to work as a teacher and researcher at the University of Veterinary and Pharmaceutical Sciences in Brno, Czech Republic. Later, I entered the pharmaceutical industry, working in senior managerial positions with an international agenda. I spent almost twenty years in the pharma industry; my

156 focus was on business planning, business development, business ethics and compliance, communication, sales, marketing, people management, and development.

I developed a unique communication/selling concept called Emotional Selling, which helps people be more effective in communication and in finding win/win solutions. Using this concept, I wrote *I Take No Sh*t*, a book that transferred these emotional selling principles to private-life situations. Though it's currently available only in Czech, it's in the process of being published in English.

In 2019, I made the biggest change in my entire life and permanently left the golden cage of corporate business to run my own business. Now through consulting, business training, and coaching, I spend my time trying to help people to have a better life.

My degrees include a doctorate in veterinary medicine (DVM), and a master's degree in business administration (MBA). I've been a baseball youth coach for ten years.

I cherish my sons Tomas and Lukas (15 and 11), and my two-year-old daughter, Agata. My fiancée and business partner, Lucie, and I live in Valasske Mezirici in the Czech Republic. I'm grateful to Lucie for her inspiration and support, without which I would never have had the courage to change my life.

Contact Information:

Email: jura.urbos@gmail.com
Facebook: Jiri Urbanek, EmocniprodejCZ
LinkedIn: www.linkedin.com/in/drjiriurbanek
Instagram: @EmocniprodejCZ
Twitter: @EmocniprodejCZ

Chapter 14

Use Every One of Your Six Senses

Tony Bryant

Growing up, my mental focus was simple: avoid pain and loneliness, stay away from negativity, hang with positive people, and never settle for being average.

I grew up in Crosby, Texas, a little town outside of Houston. Children in my low-income apartment complex were never expected to achieve more than the bare minimum life had to offer—get minimum wage jobs and survive with the help of charitable groups or welfare. Even as a child, I knew my life was *not* going to travel that path. I had ambition; I was different. I was determined to discover the way to become successful rather than become just another statistic.

My mission was to achieve more mental and monetary success than anyone I had met to that point in my life. My fear of ending up dead, in jail, broke, or unmotivated, bragging about my crowning achievements in high school athletics, would come to fruition if I didn't come up with a plan.

In my most vulnerable moments, when I knew I was in over my head, I was convinced I had to fake it until I could make it. Somehow, stretching the truth felt necessary to be part of the in-crowd. When I exaggerated, I had temporary protection from the hurtful comments of other kids and the confidence that came from feeling I had as much money and support as my peers.

> Think things through; go after whatever you believe you're capable of doing and don't rest until you reach your destination.

Growing up as a teen in the materialistic 90s was tough. I enviously watched my peers strut through what seemed to be daily fashion shows. To my eyes, they had fresh gear and the latest pair of Air Jordans for each day of the week. I was all too aware that I wore my brothers hand me downs and got Wal-Mart shoes twice a year. When I was asked about my clothes, sometimes I managed to put my chin up and say, "My value isn't in what I choose to wear." Sometimes, though, I'd lie, mumble something along the lines of, "My dad is getting even newer Air Jordans for me soon," and quickly change the subject.

I knew I was telling a boldfaced untruth as those words owed out of my mouth. My parents divorced when I was nine. My mother was a wonderful mother, and I am so grateful to her; she has the biggest heart of anyone I know. I never saw my dad contribute one penny to our household. No shoes, clothes, or anything else was ever on its way or going to come on any later date from my dad.

Not too long ago, I asked my dad why things happened the way they did, and he simply said, "I was sick." He meant his addictions; his life was focused on crack cocaine and women. Those addictions caused him to lose his decent-paying job in the chemical plants, his marriage to my mother, and his relationship with my siblings and me.

Ironically, the Air Jordans I yearned for ended up being worth less over time than what I was able to buy in those days—some Michael Jordan basketball cards. I've hung onto those cards my entire life. Somehow, my son Maddox recently managed to find them and barter a few for Pokémon cards. By accident, my childhood hobby of basketball cards turned out to be a great first investment.

As a teen, I was determined to not be lazy, get involved with drugs, participate in unnecessary drama, or settle for a dead-end job. In those days, I could have been granted access to anything negative my immature mind could imagine or desire. I could have easily been involved in quick illegal cash deals involving, crime, sex, or drugs. I was not naive to the consequences. I had a front-row seat as I witnessed classmates, neighbors,

161

my mother's boyfriend, and some of my own family members be locked up or die because of their addictions and desire to make a quick buck. Life was a struggle, but I managed to hold on to my thoughts and maintain mental control.

What was key to my survival was learning to see beyond what was right in front of me. My immediate environment gave me limited vision, and my mission was to change that, even though I didn't yet have a plan. I needed to remain optimistic in the toughest of situations. In every way, I needed to subconsciously stay awake and consciously change my dynamics. I had to develop focus and practice becoming mentally strong.

We are all capable of changing our circumstances by changing what we choose to believe. Along with having a huge amount of faith, the more we improve the quality of what we see, hear, and read eventually self-manifests. Obstacles become bumps in the road, just a natural part of our mission. I had to create a strategy to use every one of my senses to create my new reality. It was critical that wanting a better life forced me to raise my standards. I had the desire and will to change the eld of life that I played on. I had to create my vision by using what God gave me.

The brain has a variety of inputs, and I used all of them, working with every one of my senses.

Sight: I created a detailed and specific vision of what my life would look like—what I was going to own, how it looked including the exact colors, the people around me, the amount of money I would have, and all the success I was to achieve.

Touch: Visiting car dealerships and sitting in new models, driving through desirable neighborhoods, and attending open houses became part of my weekly routine. I called it dream building. It all prepared me for what my life would feel like once I reached that level.

Hear: Most of what I read, spoke about, and heard had to fuel my growth. Everyone I associated with had to speak positively, not negatively—at work, at home, with friends, or anyone with whom I af liated myself.

Taste: Occasionally, I would stretch my budget to eat at some of the ner restaurants in Houston. I wanted to know what it was like to enjoy quail, steak, and lobster served in beautiful surroundings by an impeccably professional waitstaff.

Smell: The luscious aromas of new houses, cars, and ne restaurants were going to be part of my daily life. I needed to know what those things smelled like. 163

Intuition: This bonus sense allowed me to make quick decisions, ones I didn't double-guess and that gave me con dence. In a way, my intuition navigated me to the realization of my dreams.

Once I was out on my own, I imagined the places I lived not as a scruffy apartment, but as a large and well-appointed home. I was not crazy or disillusioned, I just saw things in a different way than most people did. I ltered my vision to delete the poverty. I was hungry to achieve a better life and future. My mental wealth had to exist before my physical wealth ever could. I viewed my Pontiac Grand Am as though it were a high-end Mercedes, and I treated it that way, too.

Yes, I knew the journey would shed a few friends, and

some people would believe I thought I was better than they were, especially those who shared my background. I was ready to create the person I was to become. I was ready to lose whatever I'd already attained to gain a more positive, productive, and secure future.

Once we discover that literally, any dream is possible to achieve, our con dence matures. We then eliminate the fear of taking action, and great things can happen.

I started planning for my future while I was still in high school, dedicating my weekends to working and church. I became the head banquet waiter at the local country club. Not only did I make decent money, but I was also able to glean life tips and special bits of wisdom from the older white members who played golf and lived in what I then considered mansions.

164 As a disadvantaged teenager, I developed the skill of learning from watching the actions, successes, and failures of other people. This skill has helped me to avoid many costly mistakes and losses as I grew older. I began to understand the value of positioning, leadership, consistency, word articulation, how to self-motivate, and many equally relevant skills.

On Sundays, I spent long hours in a Southern Baptist church, often from morning until late evening, avoiding the desperate lives at my apartment complex and attempting to disassociate myself from an impoverished mentality. Sel shly, after hours in church, I sometimes fell asleep when I was supposed to be worshiping. Even asleep, my time in the church signi cantly reduced the possibility of me being around the wrong crowds or getting into trouble. I attribute my dogmatic mindset and achievements to my hours in church, staying consistently focused, praying, having vision and faith, and working hard.

By the time I was in my mid-twenties, I had put myself through college, held several leadership roles in sales and marketing management, did several real estate deals, experienced multiple business start-ups— and had many failures. I had also gained an impeccable work ethic, expert-level negotiating skills, and was sharp at nancial and operational analysis. I was also more optimistic and had some con dence in taking on new opportunities and risks.

While I knew I still had a lot to learn, I was on top of the world and felt excitement like I had never felt before. I'd known this time would come because I had manifested it several years earlier.

165

The more friends I made, the more opportunities I was offered, and most times, I believed I had to be a part of these deals even when they weren't the best investments. I went into them with my heart, not my brain—and in every case, I was sure the potential to make pro ts existed because we shared honest intentions and similar work ethics.

Over time, I discovered I didn't always pick the right partnerships. In fact, I was dead wrong in many cases, even the so-called lucrative opportunities, because my heart consistently made the wrong decisions. Experiencing so many losses took a toll on my ego, stress level, and con dence as an investor.

The year 2008 was tough for me, nancially and emotionally. In addition to my investment losses, and thanks to a reduction of 2,000-plus employees at my Fortune 500 company, my high-level career as a sales and marketing director was eliminated. Talk about adding fuel to a bonfire!

In my career, I'd already reached certain levels of success when it came to income, my role, and the impact I made. My bank account was healthy thanks to my company's payout, plus earlier real estate deals. However, none of that mattered to me because I'd always de ned myself by my career; my entire identity was wrapped up in who I was at work and the role I played for an entity in which I had no ownership.

For all these years, I'd based my self-worth and value on what I chose to do for other people and not for myself. Now, for the rst time in my life, I felt mentally stressed, even depressed. I had to nd a way to snap out of it and rediscover my mental peace and con dent performance.

I decided I was no longer going to be an employee. I never again wanted to put my energy into playing the corporate politics game or allow someone else to control my destiny. I decided to become a fulltime investor and entrepreneur. I also knew I also needed to avoid any potential investment that was barely good enough or that wasn't going to succeed. I had to put my mind back to work, not just my heart.

I was only able to do this with the full support of my lovely wife, Heather. She believed in me at times more than I believed in myself; she is my true rock and keeps me going. At that moment, I took the step that she had encouraged me to take several years earlier: I became my very own boss.

My first decision came after several months of self-evaluation and planning: We built on Heather's special talents as a dentist and opened a private dental practice. We also invested in more real estate, but only opportunities that we strongly believed in, and started several companies. At that point, I made the decision to continue to bet on and believe in myself, regardless of the situations I may face.

Twelve years after losing my job and my con dence, Heather and I own and operate a wide variety of successful businesses: dental practices, restaurant investments, trucking, a real estate investment rm, a private lending business, plus other opportunities. They all create generational wealth and allow us to add value to as many people as we can.

167

Success comes from our mind however we choose to de ne it. It cannot be achieved without a healthy, con dent mind. Most of us tend to prioritize other people, things, or careers above ourselves and what we truly need to survive mentally. If we aren't strong mentally, we limit our capabilities to visualize and deliver physically.

Being mentally healthy plays a very important role in how we interact with others, execute opportunities, and live our daily lives. Just as our bodies need proper nutrients, our brain needs to be free of stress. Exercising daily, listening to calming music, spending time in nature, reading, having interactive conversations, and eliminating unnecessary tasks, are all things that add to the valuable growth of our mental abilities and health.

We need to do all we can to eliminate the small,

irritating tasks and thoughts that don't give our lives added value. Worrying about competition, chasing fame and money, and fretting about our achievements weigh us down with huge amounts of pressure.

We aren't designed to withstand so much prolonged mental pressure. It's important to recognize we are human beings and none of us are invincible or immune to mental illness or breakdown. Do everything possible to remain mentally strong and healthy. Be responsible to yourself and take the lead position in your own growth. Life is too short to worry about things out of our control. Think things through; go after whatever you believe you're capable of doing and don't rest until you reach your destination.

I hope my humble start in life helps convince you that regardless of our backgrounds, anything is possible and we can all have strong, determined minds. We are in control of our own destinies. Life can always get better, and our best days are yet to come.

Author's Notes

Although I was born in Houston, I grew up in the nearby small town of Crosby, Texas. During my teen years, I lived with my mother and three siblings in a Section 8 low-income apartment complex. With a mainly absentee father and no mentors, role models, or clear direction, I did not know what I wanted to do with my life or what career choice to make. Instead, I knew exactly what I did not want out of life, and I did my best to avoid negative peer pressure, crime, and drugs.

169

By practicing mental discipline, I have become very successful—a millionaire by my late twenties. After serving in leadership roles in two major public companies, I left the corporate world and began my journey as a full-time entrepreneur in 2008.

I serve as the Chief Executive Officer of Home Buyers Texas LLC, a Houston-based real estate investment rm that focuses on adding value, empowering people, and improving communities. I also own and operate several other successful companies in multiple industries generating in excess of one million dollars in annual revenue: business consulting (financial/operational analysis), healthcare (dentistry), transportation (trucking), entertainment (contracts), restaurant/bars, investment education, private lending, and technology investments.

My commitment to lifelong education includes a BA in Management and MBA from the University of Phoenix, certificates in Leadership and Financial Management from the University of Houston, a Texas real estate license, and a private pilot's license.

My wife, Heather, and I live in Houston with our two daughters and two sons: Aubrey, Zarah, Maddox, and Caden.

Contact Information

Email: TonyB.Interest@gmail.com
Website: www.tonyb4profits.com
Facebook: Tony Bryant
Instagram: @tonyb4profits
Twitter: @tonyb4profits

Chapter 15

Keep Your Chin Up And Stand Tall!

Dolores C. Macias

When I was young, I swallowed a bitter pill that made me believe I was born only to endure barbaric curve balls thrown at me in the game of life. By the time I was 15, I was married, and when I was 19, I'd had my two kids and my tubes were tied. Two years later, my husband abandoned the three of us 1,300 miles from our hometown.

After another year went by, I began living with Benny, a wonderful, loving 18-year-old Mexican guy who spoke no English and who had a fourth-grade education. Two months passed, and I told him, "I'm going home to my mama and papa. Do you want to go with me?"

Benny's family thought he was crazy to move so far away with an older married lady with two little kids. Even worse, his family was very outspoken about my tubes being tied, saying it was a disgrace to the Mexican culture that he couldn't have children of his own if he went with me. But we packed the car, the four of us got in, and we left everything else behind with no regrets.

He worked hard, paid for my divorce, married me, loved me and my two kids, Monica and Rick, and adopted them as soon as he could. As our life together unfolded, it wasn't always sugarplums and daisies, though we've also had many amazing and happy times. We've had to cling tight to each other to survive 40 years and persevere through the tough times. What we've been through will make you cringe and the hairs on the back of your neck prickle.

> *You are extraordinary, and it all starts from within.*

During my son's senior year, he stopped putting forward any effort to graduate with his class. It was a battle for him to finish, and he finally graduated later that summer. This was unusual behavior for Rick, because all his life he'd been a happy, energetic, rambunctious, smart kid who loved school. After graduation, he moved out to live with friends, but they soon brought him home because he was acting weird, talking to himself, and saying the TV was sending him private messages.

This was our introduction to the horrific disease of paranoid schizophrenia. It came from nowhere but soon overtook our lives. Our son crumbled before our eyes, turning into an unknown creature, a total stranger. People called Rick insane, crazy, and a lunatic—never just an extremely ill human being. His disease led to five involuntary hospitalizations, psychiatric doctor visits, mandatory medications, and even being hauled off to jail in handcuffs.

The National Alliance on Mental Illness (NAMI) offers free classes to learn about paranoid schizophrenia, and we were glad to take advantage of them. We learned the disease is a lifelong illness with no cure. We learned about the delusions, hallucinations, distinctive movements, and many other odd things unique to this horrible disease. We learned he would have few friends if any, and that he might be unemployable. We learned Rick's whole quality of life rested in our hands as his caregivers, and we'd be responsible for his money, food, and housing.

My desire is for as many families as possible to get relief through NAMI just as I did, so for every copy of this book that's sold, I'm donating $1 directly to NAMI to help them continue to offer love and support to all who need it.

If you're willing to go further to help other humans understand or take better care of a family member with a mental illness, buy my book and promote it on your social media platforms. You can help save someone's child, sibling, parent, or friend from being thrown out into the streets because the families don't understand these difficult people are critically ill humans in crisis.

Unfortunately, Rick's illness wasn't the only cause of our pain. One night I was driving down a dark curvy road on my way home. Suddenly I strained to see something that seemed to be in the middle of the road, and *bam,* there was a bump. My heart started racing, and I asked my son, "What was that?"

He didn't know either, so I did a U-turn and went back to look at what I hit. *Omigod!* It was a person. My brain swirled, my palms sweated on the steering wheel, the hairs on my neck stood straight up. I thought, *Do I go to the corner store to call the police, or do I go home?* It was about the same distance, so I rushed home and screamed for Benny to wake up and come back with me in case they took me to jail. I called the police and returned to the site of the accident.

When I got back to the scene, though the street was blocked off by five sheriff's cars, they let me through. The deputies told me I had run over a woman, and four other cars also ran over her. She was dead. My whole body started shaking violently, and I felt something cold as ice slide down my back.

The deputies asked me over and over what happened. Each time I repeated, "I was driving around the dark curve and suddenly I saw something in the middle of the road and felt the bump. We heard no noise of any kind."

It seemed like an eternity for the investigation to take place, and we couldn't leave until it was completed. After three hours, they let us know she had been released from a nearby jail that morning, and she'd been roaming around the premises and would not leave. She was mentally ill, with no family, and had nowhere to go. They said she wanted to die and this was her suicide plan.

Her death generated a raging storm of guilt, and it consumed most of my mind, energy, and life. Quite a bit of time passed before I could eliminate the voice that kept creeping back in my mind, telling me I had killed someone. I battled post-traumatic stress for a long time.

At the same time, we were struggling financially. Benny had recently bought a $45,000 dump truck. Three weeks after my accident, a driver ran a stop sign and headed right at my husband. Though he did his best to avoid the car, his truck was hit, and he lost control and rolled over, leaving him hanging upside down in his safety belt until help came. Our new dump truck was totaled, and the driver who ran the stop sign died. Benny couldn't work for two months until everything was settled. Our finances went so far in the hole, we had to file bankruptcy.

Since that low point, we've recovered so well we are now debt-free with a credit score of over 800 and assets worth a quarter of a million dollars. I vowed not to allow my past failures, limiting beliefs, or bad circumstances to control me. I learned not to give my power away. We spend only what we have the cash for, we stick to our budget, and we save for a rainy day.

I didn't learn it easily because the past failures and bad circumstances had their hold on us. For years, my family had an unending series of traumas and problems. My dad died very suddenly and unexpectedly when he was only 64. It was painful and shocking to my whole family, and from that time, I helped take care of my mom until her death many years later.

My daughter was married at 18—her decision and most definitely *not* my wish, but I made sure Monica had a beautiful wedding. Twenty years later, with a teen

175

and two pre-teens, she divorced. Their dad then took the children away to live with him, and my daughter left our congregation, which made us very sad. I am so proud of how well our grandchildren have managed their stressful situations.

That's just the beginning of our problems and distractions. My brother is an alcoholic and panhandles to survive. My sister had a 10-pound tumor removed, and I took care of her for a long time as she recovered. Later, she—along with her diabetes, high blood pressure, and painful arthritis—permanently moved in with my husband and me.

My son's illness was finally under control and it ran smoothly for a while, then his psychiatrist decided to change his meds. Rick deteriorated quickly. He talked to the voices that only he could hear in his head. He sat staring into space for hours at a time without moving. He didn't sleep.

My husband Benny works nights, so he wasn't home at 7 a.m. the day a screeching smoke alarm woke me up. I jumped out of bed, scrambled for my shoes, and saw smoke coming out of the vent. First, I went into the bathroom, and there was thick smoke everywhere. Then I panicked, opened the bedroom door, and saw dark smoke pouring out of every vent in the house.

I hollered *"Rick!"* No answer. I ran to his room, grabbed the knob—*it was hot!* I swung the door open and fire came shooting out. The room was pitch black and I couldn't see anything. I kept screaming Rick's name but there was no sound but the crackling of the fire. I was scared, alone, and didn't know if he was in the room or not. The house seemed ready to explode.

Having no cell phone, I ran to get my purse and the cordless phone and went outside to call 9-1-1. We live on 10 acres and the driveway to the street is a quarter of a mile long. My neighbor came into the yard and said he'd seen Rick run down the driveway. I felt relief for at least I knew he wasn't burning to death. I called my husband to come home immediately and my daughter to let her know what was happening. I paced back and forth, praying until the firefighters arrived.

Can you imagine the anguish of not knowing if your son was all right? The sheriff's deputies looked for Rick for two hours before they finally found him, then he was brought to the hospital because he's a diabetic and they wanted to make sure he wasn't dehydrated.

We didn't have a stable place to stay while our house was being repaired, and we were forced to move three times in three months before it was ready for us to return home. It's hard to find a landlord who'll rent to a family with an obviously mentally ill member, much less one who is an arsonist. The state pressed charges, so now my son has a felony arson charge on his record. He ended up at the state hospital for a year and yes, he came home to live with us. Many families won't tolerate their loved ones' mental illness, which is one of the reasons there are so many schizophrenics living on the streets.

Crisis, misfortune, and overpowering circum- stances can jolt you into a world where you wonder if life is really worth living. After the fire, I fell apart internally. I was still doing my best to recover when another round of drama befell us. Benny told me his doctor wanted to see us both. We anxiously went to the office, and his doctor bluntly said, "You have cancer."

We turned and looked at each other as a chill went down my spine and my whole body began to shake. We sat there, numb, not knowing what to do, say, think, ask. We wondered, *do we cry, scream, panic? Now what?* The doctor calmly recommended surgery because Benny is young. He didn't want the tumors to ruthlessly spread from organ to organ and into his bones, squeezing life from his body. We agreed to surgery.

After surgery, my husband recovered well. His checkups were clean, but I was in so much psychological pain from the emotional roller coaster I'd been riding that I couldn't move forward. That was when we were introduced to a type of coffee with a special ingredient to help support the immune system. To my amazement, it transformed me, and I quickly began to feel happy and content.

I'd never dreamed I'd feel so good again. Benny found it enhanced his quality of life, too. Eight of our family members now drink it as well and we all feel we live and feel better. I list the URL for Organo Gold in my contact information, and I urge you to try some if you too are stressed.

Six years after Benny's surgery, the dreaded day arrived: Cancer showed its ugly head again. This time, the recommendation was 40 radiation treatments, and he's still in the process of taking them. Our spiritual family has been overwhelmingly loving and supportive as members of our congregation take turns preparing and delivering a hot meal to our doorstep. Every day, a member of our congregation picks up Benny, takes him for his treatment, waits in the car, and brings him home. We are so relieved we aren't going through this challenge alone.

We have researched how to improve the odds of a good outcome, and we discovered seed-based nutrition, which we've added to our diets. I've included the URL for Rain in my contact information because I am certain Rain is why Benny can continue to work 12-hour days with minimal side effects as he goes through his radiation treatment. I've also replaced pesky toxins that were lurking and hiding in our home with Modere products; the URL for those also is included in my contact information.

I know by now you're wondering *how does this lady* 179 *remain sane*? In the past, I felt as though I would die from all the anguish each time my heart shattered into a million pieces. It's been a heck of a wild ride.

At the beginning of this chapter, I mentioned the bitter pill I swallowed that made me believe I didn't deserve much from life and would always have the short end of the stick. The side effects of that pill shackled me for years as I went through the motions of living and pretty much just waited to die.

Now I wholly believe God does not give me more than I can bear, and that is what gives me the courage to wait for the time when He will end all suffering here on earth.

Now I pray often and read biblical accounts of how others have suffered tremendously. I'm encouraged by how God lavishly blessed them in overabundance as long as they remained faithful to him, no matter how disastrous their circumstances.

It is only through the grace of God that I courageously keep my chin up and stand *tall* to reach my golden moment. I'm eternally grateful to be healing from emotional trauma, and I long to do something for the world. I practice gratitude because I cannot be grateful and sad simultaneously. No, it is not easy, but now I can smile and have a zest for life, and my loving and supportive husband stands by my side.

Hey, look how *far* I've come!

I challenge you to get over the belief that old age means it's too late to change. If you can breathe, age doesn't matter at all in your plans to have a grand life. Life is 10% what happens to you and 90% how you react to it. Your setbacks could be *your* setup for greatness.

Stand *tall*!

Author's Notes

I was born in Austin, Texas where I've spent most of my life, and where my husband, Benny, and I live now. As an entrepreneur with several businesses, I have the freedom to work from home. Benny and I have two children, Monica and Rick, and three wonderful grandchildren, Josue, Caleb, and Franki.

Please check out my websites to find out more about my businesses; I offer you many opportunities to grow healthier and to save money while you do so. Contact me for a free code to save money on travel, seed nutrition, coffee, nutraceuticals, and toxin-free household products.

I look forward to helping and working with you.

Contact Information

Email: 1dcmacias@gmail.com
Facebook: Dolores Macias (Casarez)
Websites: www.dcmacias.myibuumerang.com
www.dcmacias.OrganoGold.com
www.rainintl.com/dcmacias
www.Modere.com/5446915

Chapter 16

Sow Your Seeds
4 a Purpose

Jené M. Patrick

My parents were drug dealers, hooked on the poison they sold. The chaotic street life I was born into didn't set me up to become a productive member of society, much less allow me to believe I could be successful.

By the time I was barely a teenager, I knew I had a choice to make. The easy choice was to become a victim of my parents' bad choices, stay in my reality of addiction and mayhem, and live a self-destructive life. Instead, I made the hard choice, to leave as soon as I could to make a new life in an environment where I'd thrive.

I share my story with you today, not for pity, but for you to understand how developing mental wealth saved me and my children for generations to come. If your story is like mine, I hope *The Power of Mental Wealth* will provide you with the tools needed to have a more fulfilling life.

The Trauma

Train up a child in the way he should go, and when he is old, he will not depart from it.
—Proverbs 22:6, **Revised Standard Version**

If I sold drugs or committed murder, you might almost expect it, excusing me, saying I was born without a chance. Luckily, God blessed me with role models, because my father was the only bad seed in his family. His sisters and my grandmother were part of my life, and they let me know my future wasn't predestined. They showed me I didn't have to follow my parents' example—I had a choice. As a

> **Words have the power of life and death.**

child it was hard to imagine, but I already knew I didn't want to live my parents' lives. I learned I *could* have the "American Dream," complete with a husband, white picket fence, and children.

My dad had his first prison stint in 1984, two years after I was born. Every time he went back to prison during my childhood, I watched as my mother waited for my father to come home and be the man she longed for. She was a beautiful young woman, and she had an essence about her that made her stand out in a crowd. Her smile lit up a room and everyone around her truly enjoyed her company. She also was a sick woman, suffering from Crohn's disease and drug and alcohol addiction.

As a parent, I know she cared for me in her own way, but when I was growing up, I felt unheard and sometimes unloved. She didn't hug us or say *I love you* often; now I realize she didn't know she should. My mother was deep in her lifestyle, so I spent my childhood caring for her and raising my two younger sisters.

As I grew, I realized she hadn't given me what I needed to feel whole; something critical was missing. For years I was just in survival mode, sweeping anything that needed to be addressed under the rug, and doing my best to cope with life. It felt as though the weight of the world was on my shoulders. As my luck would have it, that was only a small part of the weight I would later carry.

My father was both a source of strength and part of my trauma. His relationship with prison became a pattern–three years here, four years there–a pattern repeating itself for my entire life. When he was home, he was loving and I was with him as much as I could, needing his affection and attention.

But he wasn't home enough and I grew up in the prison waiting room. Whenever he went back to prison, we all visited, watching the other families like our own, taking pictures, playing games, and spending the coins my mother gave us on vending machine snacks.

185

I still can see my father crossing his legs in his unique style, propping me up on his lap as I tried to follow his flowing conversation with my mother. Like all daddy's girls, I didn't care where we were, as long as I had his presence and time.

He's now 62, doing what I *know* will be his last stint in prison, and like the true daddy's girl I still am, I really want to believe this.

Still, when I grew up there was a void that only my father could have filled. I never learned the things that a father should teach his daughter. Not having this stable relationship had consequences to me as I grew up—my choices in men, knowing how they should treat me, my value as a woman, and understanding what power I held. I had to figure it all out the hard way.

When I was 24 and a mother of three, I was diagnosed with Crohn's disease, just like my mother. I was struggling. I had just enough energy to go to work and come home, but not enough to care for my children properly. Everything I'd tried to run from was now becoming my reality. I remember telling God, "If this is life, I don't want it. Am I doomed to have the same fate as my mother?"

When I was 27, my mother became extremely ill, so I took her in and gave her full-time care for the next three years. Even then, we never talked about what hurt me as a child or about the anger I felt deep inside. I'd watched all my life as my mother's trauma led her down a self-destructive road. Life had battered and bruised her, leaving her feeling as though life had cheated her of its greatest gift.

I was 30 when she died in my home, long before her time. I'd told myself I was prepared for the moment she was gone, and then reality hit and it hit hard. I'd been lying to myself. I wasn't ready. She was dead, and I was angry, hurt, and bitter, both with her and with God.

I began to catch myself treating my children in the manner I'd sworn I would never do. I yelled like my mother, I cursed like my mother, and I gave up on life, just like my mother. My children were wounded deeply before I finally realized the consequences of what I'd learned (and not learned) from my parents.

The parental relationship is so valuable— everything that children aspire to be stems from their foundational relationship with their parents. Now I understand I was carrying the weight of multi-generational trauma passed down through my grandmother and my mother 187 to me. One of God's greatest gifts, the gift of choice, became evident to me then. It was time for me to choose: *Do I continue to follow this cycle of dysfunction and pass it down to my own children, or do I evolve into something different?*

I could use the generational trauma as a crutch and avoid evolving, but my soul craved a life that my God-given faith knew existed. The time to change and to be better had arrived, and my children and future grandchildren's lives depended on it. It was time for me to stop watering my seeds with polluted water and expect them to be great. They deserved my best, and in order to give them that, I had to repair the wounds inside me.

The Process

Now faith is the substance of things hoped for, the evidence of things not seen.

—Hebrews 11:1, **King James Version**

People are wrongly convinced that their personal growth stops when it reaches some pre-set limit. That's a lie, and don't ever let anyone tell you differently. The world is our classroom, and it's up to us to learn from our experiences. We should grow and improve over time, and we must never get too comfortable or complacent. We serve a limitless God, and we are His children made in His image, so we must know that we, too, have limitless potential for growth.

My childhood and my parenting mistakes have taught me many lessons. I've tried my best to take heed of them all, but many times I've fallen short. In fact, as I write this book, I'm battling with a decision I recently made that may detour me from God's plan. This is one of the many reasons I'm grateful for His grace and mercy. God is very intentional about what He shows us in life.

Knowing this finally led me on my healing journey. It wasn't pretty or easy, but it was necessary for my growth.

All my life, I've watched people and analyzed their actions. Whenever someone did something wrong or strange, I had to make sense of *why* they did it. I'd look at their life, their parents, and their upbringing, and come up with a logical conclusion about why they did what they did. Usually I concluded they were exposed to trauma in their childhood that shaped those actions.

This leads me to the first step in my healing journey,

forgiveness. In my hurt and anger with my mother and father, I had not given them the same understanding and grace I gave those strangers I observed.

I had to forgive my parents because holding onto my resentment prevented me from moving forward. I had to forgive because I could never expect them to give me something they didn't know how to give. Just like me, they were missing what they needed to feel whole. Just like me, they were coping the best way they knew rather than fixing the problem. I was the accidental casualty of their dysfunction. This revelation allowed me to completely forgive both my parents.

My father had a chance to try and heal from his trauma, but my mother no longer had this opportunity. I couldn't share the divine download I'd received to help her live a more fulfilling life.

189

My parents never hurt me intentionally. Neither did yours! Work on your wounds for yourself, your family, and for the life you want. When we really dig deep, we will find that we have been the one damaging others in our *own* brokenness. We often excuse our own actions because we were "done wrong," but that still doesn't make them right.

If you're always angry, resentful, and in survival mode, it's time to heal, because you're cheating yourself and your family out of a full and rewarding life. Those who hurt you probably felt justified for their actions and didn't know better, so forgive them. Just don't forget to forgive yourself at the same time.

The process of forgiveness is not easy, and I don't mean to make it seem easy. Doing this work on yourself requires you to open wounds you thought were already healed. It may even bring you to dark places. The darkness doesn't last; we must do the challenging work first and get mentally and physically healthy so we can care for those around us.

Healing from any trauma is messy business. At some point you'll question the process and wonder if you're torturing yourself instead of healing. Just remember that it's necessary before you can reach your destination. You'll feel you're traveling though wilderness; acknowledge that feeling, because walking this road can only be done by faith. The Lord already promised you the victory; you just have to make the journey.

While you're on this healing journey, you can expect to feel the most misunderstood and even the most hurt that you've ever been in your life. You'll get crazy looks, you'll be accused of acting funny, and often you'll feel out of place where you once felt comfortable.

As you transition into the new you, your circle will naturally become smaller and more intimate. You'll learn that not everyone will continue a relationship with you. You'll expect certain people to leave, but the absence of some will knock the wind out of you. You'll learn they had actually kept you from moving forward, because no one enables your b.s. more than those closest to you.

God is intentional about the contact you have with others. As your growth changes you, the people who stay around you are those He assigns to help you in your journey. These people will be motivating and inspiring.

You'll have many *ah-ha!* moments in this phase, and you'll have a glimmer of hope of what the future can hold for you and those close to you. Just don't get too comfortable yet.

Boundaries are your next step. Nothing can halt your growth faster than someone toxic whom you love. It doesn't matter who it is—mom, dad, sister, brother, cousin, girlfriend, or grandma—you need to keep away from their poison.

No will be your new best friend. Saying "no" was and still is a struggle for me. People-pleasing was my normal pattern, so saying no was gut-wrenching. People are in the habit of having you fill their needs, but now *you* need *you*. You must maintain a hedge of protection while you are fixing yourself. Trust the process. 80% of the answers you give will be *no*, and that's okay! You're fixing yourself. Saying no doesn't mean you don't love them; love and pray for them from afar.

It's hard to imagine at this point, but your healing is not just about you—it's *bigger* than you. Your work and your healing create a bonus: Not only do you thrive, but you're helping others thrive as well. Some of your toxic friends and family will discover that your healing has become the start of *their* breakthrough.

Now that you have forgiven people, created boundaries, and learned to say no, it's time to humble yourself and see where *you* are the problem. How do you talk to yourself? Are you speaking positivity, life, and abundance to yourself?

Words have the power of life and death, especially the words we speak to ourselves. Along your journey, sometimes you'll have to depend on just *you* to speak life into yourself, and this will keep you safe and strong when you're in the dark spaces. Your own words will remind you that you're worthy, powerful, and resilient.

Go to your bible and see what God says about the words we speak. When you need a word of encouragement from your Father, Google will become your best friend and lead you to the passage that specifically fills your need. I have fallen asleep many times reading God's words about me, and the revelations were truly amazing.

Let's review more steps on the journey:

Acknowledge your actions. This is the first step. Admit that in your brokenness you neglected things and people.

Hurt people hurt people. We have all heard this before, but by this point you should start to see where your own brokenness causes you to hurt people you love. In my case, I'd hurt my children.

Apologize. I was very open and honest with my daughters about generational trauma and my growth.

Change your actions, or your acknowledgement and apology means nothing. From the moment I apologized, I made sure they witnessed the changes I was making. I modeled a new way of being for them, and that superseded anything I was doing for myself. I know my actions determine my daughters' outcomes. What I model, they mimic. Being intentional about changing their perception about me and who I was becoming was imperative. My mission is to witness them growing into healthy, whole adults. They are a part of my legacy.

In closing, I pray that the words I share resonate

within your spirit. I hope you understand your mental health and mental wealth are key factors in having a fulfilling life. Self-improvement should be part of your life until the day you die; you'll never reach the end of that road.

Embrace it all! Enjoy the ride, tell your story to help others, and find the peace you so deserve.

Author's Notes

We get one shot at life. When we are born, death is the only certainty, but how we live is a choice. My choice is to be the change I want to see in my home, in my community, and in the world.

As a community advocate, I work in a leadership role with Mothers of Murdered Columbus Children. I use my voice to help others by telling my story and talking about overcoming generational trauma.

The owner of Seeds Speaking and Coaching, I teach organizational change management and coach women on reaching their highest potential. As the keynote speaker at community events and churches, I share my message on being the change. In 2022, I founded a nonprofit, Seeds 4 Purpose, with a goal of helping those who feel trapped due to unhealed trauma.

I live in Columbus, Ohio, with two of my three beautiful daughters, Jazmond, 15, and Joel, 14. Jaden, 20, serves in the Air Force and is stationed in Guam.

Contact information:

Email: jene@seeds4purpose.com
Website: Seeds4purpose.com
Facebook: Jené Monique Patrick
Instagram: planted_by_faith

Chapter 17

Falling Doesn't Count; Getting Back Up Does

Darren McKevitt

I reland, my home, is a small island with a lot of heart and potential. I believe the Irish people are evolving more and faster now. We have great men and women who are smashing their self-limitations and personal beliefs and becoming whomever they choose to be.

It took me a while to get to that point, though. At a noticeably young age, I developed a negative mindset. I had no mental wealth or focus and never felt as if I was *enough*. A lot of the bad habits I developed came from my family's beliefs and perceptions and the environment around me. I grew up in a broken home. My father was not around much. Alcohol, drug abuse, and crime were his way of life, so I was raised by my working mother, who struggled to hold down a job and care for me.

It wasn't always bad—there were good, happy times as well. When my father was around, you could see that beneath all the baggage and tough exterior, there was a strong love. But that didn't offset what was happening all around me while I was growing up.

My hometown was flooded with heroin. Every night there was always something chotic happening on the road—if it wasn't car chases or joyriding, it was stabbings and shootings. Mostly, though, it was ego-based arguments over who was better than whom. (Apparently, they thought they had their reputations to uphold.) Growing up, that was my normal, and I had unknowingly become a

You alone can do it, but you can't do it alone.

product of my environment. Now, don't get me wrong—I had a part to play in all of it. I loved the madness! But why did I love it?

When I was eight years old, I had my first trouble with the law. I was caught with a sports bag full of sweets, crisps, and cakes taken from a local shop. As you can see, even at that age, I wasn't settling for mediocre. I wanted it all or nothing. My wildness continued as I got older. I started smoking hashish when I was 10, and by 11, I was selling drugs.

By then, I had experienced my family's struggles as we scraped by, my mother working a hard job, five days a week, and having nothing to show for it beyond our living expenses. My mother made sure I was cared for properly and did it well and on her own. Throughout all of it, she stuck to her morals, but I didn't want that for my future. By then, I had witnessed how easy it was to make money in different ways and I saw the lifestyle having money can bring.

I wanted it.

I wanted *all* of it, no matter what the outcome might be.

Growing up, I was a terribly angry child. I had witnessed a lot of violence in my home and community. When I didn't live up to my own personal standards, I would turn it inward and criticize myself in a horribly negative way that in turn left me feeling like an empty shell. My ego was damaged, and I felt worthless, so I countered that feeling by engaging in bad behavior as my escape, which was my way of deflecting pain.

By 15, I had lost a limb while stealing a motorbike. [197] I was always stealing. I had to—I needed the buzz, the excitement of it. Every time my mother and I would go out to shops, I would fill my pockets, and *boom!*—the thrill would hit me.

That is where my self-worth, self-talk, self-belief, self-perception, and self-discipline went out the window along with any bit of backbone I had left. I had no self-discipline whatsoever. I felt very vulnerable—quite different from most people I knew.

After losing a part of my body through my own actions, I was bombarded with horrible thoughts and feelings. My friends and I would joke about it, but subconsciously it was affecting me on a deeper level. I was being hit by the full gambit of disempowering thoughts like *you're not whole, you're weak, you can't do this, you're less than everyone else.*

The thoughts brought on a lot of fear and even more fearful thoughts. It became repetitious and created a cycle of anxiety. In response, I began to take more drugs and commit more crimes. As the years went on, my mind was consumed by negative messages and my world grew worse as negative opportunities would present themselves. There was crime, violence (against me or someone I knew), drugs, parties, and a lot of hate talk against me or someone I knew.

By the time I was 20, I was addicted to pills, cocaine, weed, alcohol, sex, and crime. My diet was terrible—I can't recall a full week of healthy eating. I was always eating takeout food and eating it too quickly and at unreasonable times and in unreasonable amounts. I chose food for the flavor, with no care for nutrition.

198

At every moment, I was selling drugs and anything else I thought to be profitable, constantly chasing money. The obsession was there, along with the drive and desire, but the more I chased money, the more it ran from me. I had no money management skills whatsoever, no structure, and no self-discipline or self-control. As I turned 21, I got myself into a lot of debt with multiple drug dealers, the police were all over me, and my life seemed to spiral out of control.

I lost everything but still had an unstoppable ambition to do better and get out of my mess. I had a vision in my head of me being wealthy but nothing else beyond that. I signed myself into rehabilitation to get myself together and become a different person. The Christian drug rehabilitation center was my first attempt to do some work on myself. During my three months in rehab, I had a spiritual intervention. It was inexplicable to me at the time, but I knew something had changed within me.

As time went on, I fell back into the trap of drug abuse, negative thinking, and out-of-control behavior. I was not being consistent with my new behaviors and habits. Hospitals, jail, and rehab became my new habits, and I would delude myself into thinking I could have a positive life while behaving and speaking critically of others and most of all, myself.

After doing a lot of reflection while I was in the hospital, I decided to change my life. I was a 28-year-young man and had nothing to show for it. I could see my vision and what I desired moving further and further away. I decided to go ALL in, with no half-measures. I realized that no matter what we do in life, we must give it 100 percent or it won't work. So, I took everything I had learned from over the years and started to apply it.

When you are on a journey to spirituality, to change, to make money, or whatever it is, if the small little daily habits of self-evolution are consistently attained, well, then, our outer world will also change. Think of it like playing snooker. If you are off by a millimeter when hitting the ball, the outcome will be a major change in direction at the end.

While I was in the hospital contemplating life, an opportunity presented itself to change my whole life, and that was to go back into therapy—a therapeutic community, which means therapy 24 hours a day, 7 days a week. At first, I turned my nose up at the opportunity because I already had been through therapy, thank you, and I thought, "I'm not doing *that* again."

After doing more thinking, I realized I had to drop my ego, be humble, and admit defeat once again. I did some research on the facility where the therapy would take place and found it to be the perfect place to heal myself mentally, emotionally, physically, and spiritually.

It turns out I have a knack for psychology, philosophy, and self-development. *I love this.* The fact that you can become the type of person you want to be just by changing your behavior is fascinating. Trying to figure out life is appealing to me. I want to learn more about life; how it works, and how thoughts and behaviors can make our reality. Now my vision has become a lot clearer: I want to give back; I want to help individuals like myself who were stuck in a rut. I want to change their minds!

You must give back whatever you took from life. What that means is whatever you benefited from, whether materials, emotions, or knowledge, you must pay it forward. I wanted freedom. I wanted a good and honest life where I held myself accountable for everything that happened to me during my life, including the bad choices that I chose to make.

Everything you go through in life is for your benefit. When you figure that out, you will master life.

When I got out of rehab, after doing 18 months, I was a new man but I found myself in the same world. I still was in the early stages of recovery, and I started from rock bottom with a fresh mindset. Money was the

200

furthest thing from my mind because I wanted to learn more about *myself.*

Success is about achieving your goals, overcoming addictions and vices, and taking whatever is thrown at you as you keep moving forward.

One of my toughest vices to overcome is that when things get tough, I sulk, I don't get anything done, and I will throw my toys out of my baby carriage, metaphorically speaking. I get angry and revert to what was always comfortable. I'll eat unhealthy food and I do harmful things that stop me from progressing.

Look at it like this: A business takes one to three years of build-up to be successful. Building yourself up from scratch to fully become who you want to be, takes the same amount of time. So why are we so scared to fail along the way?

Most people will not succeed because they don't want to be seen failing, or they are afraid to step out of their comfort zone. But there is a whole other world waiting just outside the window if you allow yourself to see it.

To be successful is to fail multiple times. As Johnny Wimbrey says, just swing the bat; it doesn't matter if you miss, just swing and get going. Let go of perfectionism because it will literally stop you from moving forward.

One year after being out of rehab, I was still very much getting used to what life as a different person is like. At that point, I decided to get going with making my theories into my new reality. I got out the laptop and began to write. As time went on, procrastination began to set in and all these self-limiting thoughts filled my head: *Who am I to think I can do this? Who do I think I am? I will never be able to this?* Fear sat in and blinded me from seeing the way through. I had an *I can't* attitude. The funny thing about all of this is that it's just in my head.

I developed a morning routine—a 4 a.m. wake-up followed by hypnosis, yoga, and meditation, then going straight into a cold shower. The routine was giving me a clearer mind, but not only that, I was handling the problems life was throwing at me without taking them so personally. But again, I wasn't consistent, and I went at it on and off for ages.

Despite my lapses, I really did realize there was absolutely nothing to stop me from achieving the lifestyle I aspired to, no matter what. That obsession was getting stronger. No matter how many times I failed, I always got back up and moved forward, getting further than my last attempt.

Finally, I built a resilient mindset. I looked at every role model out there and adopted their habits. I got rid of everything that wasn't serving me or the lifestyle I wanted to achieve. I became extremely grateful for everything in my life and realized the power of giving back. As time went on, I added more micro-habits and began growing more self-sufficient with a well-developed *I can!* mindset.

To build mental wealth, we must first push through our mental challenges and build enough self-confidence to achieve any goal. Yes, it's a struggle to utilize the importance of micro-habits and to put them into daily practice. Yes, we fall, and sometimes we stay down. *I have*—thousands of times. It's a matter of finding the power that's buried deep within and letting that bugger come back stronger than before. When we accomplish anything in life, either small or big, we must congratulate ourselves and pat ourselves on the back.

You alone can do it, but you can't do it alone.

You must become self-aware, and by doing so, look out for the patterns that occur *before* you fall. This can prevent you from staying down when you fall, or even falling at all. The more you bounce back from the shit life can throw at you, the quicker you can get back on track. The most important thing to look at is that we grow and learn from our failures.

A great way to change or reframe a situation from a negative to a positive is by saying *I love it!* and then doing your best to *mean it.* For example, fear would set in whenever I thought of writing. My fear blocked me mentally, but the more I told myself I loved it, the more I was able to break free and actually fall in love with it.

A strong person is held accountable for his actions, not his voice. We need to hold ourselves accountable for every little thing in life, including words, no matter the circumstance. As time goes on, the obstacles that looked big start to become small. Fear does not have a presence anymore and we begin to move forward quickly.

We can adapt to a winner's mindset by broadening our perception of what success is because success means different things to each of us. I believe reinventing ourselves by gaining new skills is the only way to get free from that stuck-in-history version of ourselves we probably imagine. Our brains are like software; if they aren't updated regularly, we become less useful. When we regress in life, we can reverse the direction. No matter what we want to change can be changed, from habits to traits to personality disorders.

We can become anyone we want to be, *but only if we do the work.* Our reality is formed by our perceptions, beliefs, and habits. We cannot fully step into a new world unless every part of us is changed; otherwise, it would be like putting a cassette into a CD player.

Through self-awareness, daily practice of growth challenges, and putting your true self first before anything, our self-esteem—our power—begins to rise.

Author's Notes

I was born on Halloween, on the southside of Dublin, Ireland, to a family that was quite small, to be honest.

After my early years of crime and addiction, I made the conscious decision to change my life. My rehab was 18 months long, including an extra three months I believed I needed.

205

Now that my whole mindset has changed, the opportunities that are presented are good, positive, fun, and safe. Everything I've learned over the years, including the tools I gained in therapy, helps me level up challenges with an I-can attitude, no matter what is thrown my way. I understand the challenges are for my benefit, which enables me to use them to my advantage.

The people in our lives change us and reflect us. This is why I was so honored to be chosen as a co-author by the world's best multi-millionaire coach and best-selling author of *Building a Millionaire Mindset*, Johnny Wimbrey, along with the world's number one motivational speaker Les Brown, and the marketing and woman's empowerment guru, Heather Monahan.

I'm now certified in holistics coaching, specializing in hypnotherapy, and help people to start and scale a six- to seven-figure online business. These are things people dream of—and through hard work and sacrificing your old life, such dreams are possible.

So, dream big and go for it without fear.

Contact Information

Email: info@darrenmckevitt.com
Website: www.darrenmckevitt.com
Facebook: Darren Mckevitt
Instagram: @darren.mckevitt
Twitter: @THEIRISHALCHEMIST

Chapter 18

Lessons From My Father
Trials will make you stronger

Linda Nefertiti

If you are going through hell . . . don't stop!
—Johnny Wimbrey

My earliest memory is still painful after all these years. When my elementary school teacher molested me in a darkened classroom, he changed my life. My teacher was an authority gure I had been taught to trust, and he violated that trust when he violated my young body and mind.

After I told my mother, she went to the school to confront him, a white man, and he denied my story, saying, "There's no way I would have touched a little nigger girl!" The principal backed him up, and they both said I was a troublemaker. By the time my mother left the of ce, she was repeating everything they had drilled into her head. I was doubly violated; the one person who was supposed to protect me let me down, too. I was left to fend for myself. In addition to losing my innocence, I lost my ability to trust authority, which led me to a myriad of problems.

" Sometimes the smallest things can have the greatest impact on life

As I built layers and layers of walls around myself and tried to keep people from getting close to me, I lost my trust in everyone. By the time I graduated from high school, I had been raped and abused again. My boyfriend tried to kill me while I was pregnant, and then I tried to end my own life.

Fortunately, God had plans for me and my unborn child, and my firstborn son Akiiki was born in April 1973.

In the 1970s, I became good friends with my husband-to-be, and I knew immediately we were meant to marry. He had a daughter just six months older than my son and we had a rough time blending our families at first, but thank God we did. We moved to Houston and were married in 1979. Two years later, we had a son (Hodari) together and became one big, happy family.

When the children spent the summer of 1987 in Michigan with their grandparents, there were complications on the return trip. I ended up having to fly to Detroit to pick up my five-year-old son, whose ticket had been misplaced by the airline. Heading back,

Continental Airlines had problems with our plane and rerouted Houston passengers onto Northwest Airlines Flight 255. I hated to fly in the first place, and after almost 13 hours at the airport, I was tired, frustrated, and refused to get on that plane with my son.

The other Houston-bound passengers boarded, took off—and moments later, we heard the plane crash and break apart. All passengers were killed except a four-year-old girl. I was terri ed because I still didn't realize all the miracles God had already worked in my life.

Dig Deeper

In 2003, my husband was diagnosed with multiple myeloma, a rare and deadly cancer, and given only 11 months to live. During the seven years he survived, he always tried to make a difference in the lives of others. [209] The day before my 56th birthday, he took his last breath. He fought a good fight and will forever be loved and remembered.

After he died in 2010, I started attending a neighborhood church, and even though I was not a member, I was asked to lead a small group. I agreed. For our study book, I chose *Dig Deeper*, by Nigel Beynon and Andrew Sach, not only to understand God's word better but to dig deeper into who I was. I had to uncover wounds that had been buried deep inside of me and had festered in my soul for decades.

I went about my daily life as if nothing was wrong; my lifelong tendency to hide pain gave me the ability to project strength. My sons knew I was suffering, but they were the only ones. At night I would lie across my bed and cry myself to sleep.

As I watched Oprah's show one night in 2011, Tyler Perry was talking about Oprah giving Morehouse College scholarships to 300 young African-American men. These young men were becoming doctors, lawyers, business owners—men of substance—thanks to Oprah paving the way.

I sat straight up in bed and told God I wanted to do something of that magnitude. I prayed and asked him to send me a vehicle that would help me nancially and would allow me to make a difference in the lives of hundreds of others. A few days later, a friend of mine invited me to see a presentation and meet a couple who would change my life forever. They are still in my life and making a difference today, and I thank God for Edwin and Andrea Haynes.

210

Goal-Getting Sisters

Every Queen needs a tribe.
—Earlene Buggs

I formed a bond with a Mastermind group of women called Goal Getters and joined the group. As women with similar experiences, we set goals in the areas of business, nances, relationships, health, and spirituality.

One of my goals was to lead another small group, hoping it would bring me on a closer path to God. For our study book, I chose *Undaunted*, a book on human trafficking, written by Christine Caine. As I led the group, I decided to share my story. I was amazed at how quickly they all opened up and shared experiences they had never told anyone else! The book helped us strengthen our relationship with God. I was excited to learn several of them in turn became small group leaders and were also able to make a difference.

Visualize it, believe it, and you will have it

*In life you don't get what you
want, you get what you picture.*
—Holton Buggs

Best-selling author! dominates the center of one of the many vision boards hung throughout my condo. I've followed Johnny Wimbrey over the years; when we met in December 2019, we took a picture together, [211] and I posted it on Facebook. Amazingly, today I'm co-authoring a book with Johnny, who's a best-selling author several times over. I used to fear ying, and now I feature the word *Travel* at the top of the same vision board. Since then, I've traveled to several international destinations and am part of a technology company that offers travel as its first vertical.

Early this year, I woke up one morning at 3 a.m. and found my vision board had fallen off the wall. When I picked it up, I was surprised at what I saw; in fact, I don't remember putting it on the board. But when I saw these words, I knew God was telling me what my purpose was: "It's been 10 years and 100 women making a beautiful difference in 1000s of lives."

The words made sense to me. My husband had died

ten years before. In my first book, I wrote, "My purpose is to help 100 families earn a seven-figure income and change the financial fabric of their lives, while we enrich the lives of thousands around the world." Now I realized I could do this by helping 100 women.

Though it made sense, it shocked me because I'd never wanted to be a part of a big group of women. I now understand I am supposed to lead and guide 100 women . . . it must be part of God's divine order because that is clearly not something I would ever endeavor to do on my own.

I was once a member of a woman's group called Nzinga, in the Shrine of the Black Madonna. I recently reconnected with Gail Carr (Bayo), the group leader, and my former mentor, and she gave me a picture showing me standing in front of the group, as though I was leading. I have no idea when this picture was taken, but it was prophetic. Gail, who was once my mentor, has joined the technology business team that I lead.

Isolation can bring about inspiration

You are whole and complete no matter what anyone else thinks of you.
—Lisa Nichols

After my husband's death, I found out for the first time what it was like to live alone. My condo is just 800 square feet, just the right amount of open space for me—a person with claustrophobia—to feel comfortable in. I was blessed to have the condo, for after his death I lost everything except my mind, and sometimes that was questionable. Moving into this condo helped me rebuild my life and my credit. I rode the bus and rented cars until I was able to afford a new vehicle. God gave me back everything I lost a hundred-fold, and now I'm driving a vehicle I have wanted for years, an Audi.

Living alone, awakened my creativity, and writing this poem was one of the results:

Queendom

We're encouragers and nurturers, among other things,
Goal-getting sisters, you know what I mean,
Nifty fifty, below and above,
A shoulder to lean on, we'll give you much love.
But don't get it twisted, our families we'll defend,
We're determined and on purpose, on us, you can depend.
We'll bend, but our motto is, you'll never get the best of me.
Instinct plus purpose together leads to destiny.
Goal-getting sisters, go build your Queendom, girls!
Change yourself first, then go change the world!

213

Last March, I left the office, took an empty elevator— and it suddenly stopped on the sixth floor. I pushed the alarm and tried to open the door. The inside door opened all the way, but the outside door opened just enough to let some air in.

Remember, I'm claustrophobic. Trying not to panic, I yelled and screamed, and three people came to my rescue. They couldn't get me out, and then the maintenance man discovered the elevator cable had broken. He told me how to turn the power off so that the elevator would not move again. Then he explained I was blessed that the elevator stopped on the sixth floor rather than plunging to the bottom floor.

It was clear I was about to be stuck in the elevator for hours and I had to make a decision. If I panicked like I normally do in a claustrophobic situation, I could have sent my blood pressure up, gone into convulsions, had a stroke—or worse, had a heart attack. I took deep breaths and called my accountability partner, Belivian Carter. She helped me create the condition in my mind that allowed me to visualize myself on the other side of the elevator door.

Then I called my prayer partner, Sundra Woodfolk (Adero); she prayed for me and continued to tell me to trust God. I sat down on the oor and stayed calm— and then the remen showed up and turned out all the lights! Then they had to close the door! I thank God that I was able to keep my composure. I made it through my time in the elevator without incident.

Change is constant; my life experiences have helped me through some extremely rough times, but all glory belongs to God for the things he has brought me through! I have been constantly improving because of the books I read, the things I listen to, and the associations I have.

Recently I attended *Rise up Challenge*, a power-packed virtual summit put together by Pete Vargas, where 60 different world in uencers spoke and poured wisdom into all of the participants. I'm extremely grateful to all the speakers in that summit for sharing their knowledge. One of those speakers was the motivational speaker and best-selling author, Les Brown. Now I am not only collaborating with Mr. Brown on this book, I am also part of his Power Voice speaker group.

In 2017, I made a conscious decision to be transparent and allow others to look at the adversities I'd experienced that still held me back. My chapter in *Positive Mental Attitude* included very personal testimonies, and once I shared them, I thought I could look forward to a brand-new life where I never needed to mention those terrible experiences again. I said I was an overcomer, and I expected everything to come up smelling like roses!

The problem was, I never dealt with the root of the problems, not until I wrote this chapter in *The Power of Mental Wealth.*

Though I had exposed my demons, I had not let them go. I've always been an encourager for other people, but there was a flip side to my positivity. I was strong because of the anger pinned up inside of me, because of my past hurts.

215

For the last several years, I have worked to make a difference. I continue to ask God to use me in a mighty way to show that he uses imperfect people for his Glory. I know he isn't through with me yet!

I have mentored young girls who are leaving middle school, heading into high school, and I am able to speak and share my story. This has helped some girls to open up to me about their experiences. It is fulfilling to be able to let them know they can make a difference and can be anything they put their minds to. I have also worked with women to make a difference in their lives, by sharing some of my story and my vision to help women.

Now I feel I am strong because I know who I am, *whose* I am, and what my purpose is. For the first time, I can see the root of the problem. In a recent conversation with my coach, he said these words and they stuck with me, *"Stop trying to do God's job!"*

At first, the words took me aback and gave me pause, but then I realized what he was saying. I always wanted to control whatever took place in my life. I believe everything happens for a reason and things do not manifest in our time. God is always in control!

My father taught me survival skills

Behind every challenge lies opportunity.
If you lament too long over the challenge
you will miss the opportunity.
—Edwin Haynes

On May 28, 2020, my 91-year-old father succumbed to cancer. He had served in the Korean War in the Army's 82nd Airborne Division as a paratrooper. He did two tough tours of duty between 1946 and 1954, and after serving his country, he moved us to Detroit, Michigan where he opened up Roger's Barber Shop. My dad employed many people from the community, again giving service.

When he died, racial tension was as bad as during the Detroit riots of 1967, when police lined the streets and we had to stay in the house because the community was lled with violence. It felt like déjà vu.

During the pandemic, we couldn't visit him because he was quarantined. My father let my other sisters know he was ready to transition; however, my youngest sister and I did not get to see our father before he made his transition. He tried to hold on until we arrived, however, when they told him our planes had landed safely he took his last breath. We were able to witness him being honored on a flag-covered bed, with the Veteran's Walk of Honor. Hearing the words, "Honored veteran leaving the floor," filled me with pride. He was my first mentor and hero and introduced me to the network marketing industry. Shortly after my father passed away, I learned some things about him I hadn't known, which taught me some things about myself as well.

With my father's death, my life was once again turned upside down. His death was not one of sadness, though; I drew strength from writing his obituary, and I knew I had to continue the legacy both he and my late husband left.

217

The realities of what happened with my father and the world-wide virus made me snap back to it. In all, I lost five family members and four friends within four months. On the other hand, I was blessed to gain Charity, my 28-year-old granddaughter whom I'd never met before but am now getting to know. I thank God that He gave me a strong constitution, a high tolerance for pain, and the power of mental wealth to push through and complete the journey that is set before me.

Author's Notes

As the third-oldest daughter of nine children born to Roosevelt and Mablene Rogers, family has always been important to me. I am grateful to still have my mother with me at the age of 89; she taught me how to persevere and maintain a strong faith in God.

My family also consists of my sons Akiiki (my rock), and Hodari (my music); a stepdaughter, Tishauna; two granddaughters, Charity and Akila; three grandsons, Jayden, JayVaughn, and Jaymarri; and a great-grandson, Ayden, who stole my heart. I love to sing, dance, make others laugh, travel, and write poetry. Tai chi and yoga also help me relax.

Though my formal education ended at high school graduation, I have gained a wealth of knowledge and a thirst to continue learning. I continue to participate in the network marketing industry because it offers personal self-development with a compensation plan attached and affords everyone an equal opportunity to succeed. For 35 years, I've worked in the financial and insurance industry, and I realize I enjoy it because of the service we render to others.

I dedicate my chapter in this book to the memory of my father, Reverend Roosevelt Rogers, Jr., and my late husband of 35 years, Robert (Hodari) Patton.

Contact Information

Email: Lpatton11@hotmail.com
Facebook: Linda Nefertiti Patton
Instagram: @lnefpatton
Twitter: @Lpattons11
LinkedIn: Linda Patton

Chapter 19

Rising From the Ashes

Carolyn M. Johnson

"Why don't you just go out and get a job!" I can laugh at those words now, but I said them pretty loudly and snidely when my cousin, Bob Schmidt, first invited me to join him in network marketing. I was in my 20s and just launching a career in real estate. My life had been tough up to that point and I knew nothing came easily, especially money.

In my youthful and too-certain opinion, success and wealth were the results of having a really good job—or better yet, owning a brick-and-mortar business. Whatever Bob was pitching, I wasn't going to have any part of it. I rather rudely declined his offer and put it out of my mind.

It's funny how life changes. As it evolves, you shift the way you see the world.

A couple of decades passed, and cousin Bob reappeared. He was looking healthy, happy, and exceptionally well-to-do. He'd been living an extravagant lifestyle, the fruit of his smart labor and the testament to his immense professional success. There I was, still in the same town, still grinding away hour after hour. To be sure, I had enjoyed a certain level of success and achieved goals I'd set out to accomplish. I'd climbed the corporate ladder and even owned my own small business.

However, at that moment I was also drowning under a burdensome debt after the failure of a big stadium event I'd created and produced. Twice divorced, I was upside down, had sold my home, liquidated my assets, and was renting a ten-by-twelve-foot bedroom

If you are ready to move forward in your life, I offer my hand to help you up.

from a friend as I repaid enormous debts for which I'd assumed full responsibility.

It was all too apparent that my decades of diligent efforts, ambitious aspirations in the corporate world, and my own business had never given me any true financial freedom—and especially not freedom of my time. On the other hand, Bob was enjoying both; he had far more time and money than rightly seemed fair. He patiently encouraged me to take another look at network marketing. I finally realized I could trust Bob's leadership, and that time I did. I was ready to rise from the ashes.

222

When I remember the tiny rented room where I launched my new business, with space just for a bed, a dresser, and a computer table in the corner, I'm humbled and amazed at how far I've come.

Bob was serious about business, and I earnestly followed his guidance. I put his system in place, immediately began to make money, and began to retire my debt, a healthy chunk at a time. With Bob's direction, I laid out a clear business plan, and every single day, week after week, I progressed.

Within three years, my network marketing business efforts were more than amply rewarded. I was earning a *seven-figure* income—more money than I'd made *in total* during the first 14 years of my corporate career—and I did it from home with no employees and no inventory. I repaid my debts in a third of the scheduled time, and I bought a million-dollar home. 223

For many, it's hard to believe that you can start with no promises, no salary, no insurance, and no paid vacations—and end up creating a success rarely achieved as either an employee or a small business owner. *Seven* figures. *Three* years. Stunning.

Does that happen to everyone? Of course not. But my "why" was great, and I was serious and dedicated. I had good reason to rise from the ashes again. I knew the worst and wasn't about to relive it.

As a young girl, I grew up in the scathing heat of my father's perpetual anger and disappointment in life, and most directly with me. He wasn't a gentle person to begin with; he was prone to drinking way too much, and he had wanted a boy. He'd had three girls and

I was the one he said should have been a boy... that my bedroom should have resembled my boy cousins' room . . . bats, balls, and gloves. It was hurtful and confusing when I was very small; my very presence seemed to make him angry and I could never please him. His scorn and cruelty drove me to search out others whom I could please instead: others' parents, priests, nuns, and most particularly, Jesus Christ himself. In my young mind, I thought if I could just make everyone happy, they—*and my father!*—wouldn't be filled with anger all the time.

I did continue to try to keep my father from becoming angry, though. God had given me a powerful will, but no amount of effort worked with my father, not kind words, being good, laughter, or hard work—none of it. Certainly, there were occasional happy moments in my childhood, like anybody else's, but the fear of being attacked emotionally and verbally constantly hunted me.

Abuse and alcoholism had run rampant through generations of my family, along with a patriarchal view of women and their place. College was for men; making babies was for women. Women shouldn't aspire to do the things men did. Being brought up to believe I was a constant disappointment to my father and family gave me a rampaging case of low self-esteem. The insults lived forever in my brain: *You're not pretty! You're not smart enough to do that! You will never amount to anything!*

I worked hard from the age of 14, keeping my head down, trying to please people, and do a good job. As soon

224

as I graduated from high school, my world was upended when my mother escaped from her unhealthy marriage with my little sister in tow—leaving me behind.

At that time, I gave up. I was exhausted and I stopped trying to please everyone—even God, even myself—mostly my father.

As I looked at my prospects, and my father's expectations, college was never an option. I was supposed to get married and have babies—plain and simple. I did, however, make my father happy when I married an alcoholic just like him, an abusive 31-year-old, a chip off the old block. At 19, it was the only way I imagined I could both escape and please my father, and it was a classic case of jumping out of the frying pan into the fire.

My first marriage was turbulent in such a painful ^{225} way that I search for words to describe it. Looking back, it's obvious it was a foregone conclusion that I would find myself tangled in cruel abuse again. It was something I had grown accustomed to from an early age, and although often terrifying, it was somehow perfectly normal. In my marriage, though, there wasn't just verbal abuse; my husband physically intimidated and hurt me as well.

After I had my beautiful baby girl, Cathryn, I escaped because I was not going to allow her to live a childhood filled with fear and lack of self-worth, as I had. When Cathy was almost five years old, I reunited with my high school sweetheart. We moved to Phoenix, Arizona, to be married and started over. Yes, I tried to go back to the good old days. The problem was, there weren't any good old days in my past.

While I managed to change my surroundings and my companion, I had brought *myself* with me, which included my view of the world and my place in it. My life couldn't completely change until I changed my views. What went on inside my head is as important as whatever happened on the outside.

My second marriage also had no chance of survival, and we divorced for the same reasons we broke up years before in high school: two different people, two different priorities, and the inability to communicate. Fortunately, something good came from our marriage, a handsome baby boy, Thomas. I'm blessed to work alongside Tommy in business today.

It was rather fortuitous that I found myself in Phoenix for my first and second acts of rising from the ashes. When I think of the symbolism of the *phoenix*, a universal symbol of rebirth and renewal, that fabled bird rising from the ashes, I realize God might have been up to something.

My life and struggles—a story of fall and recovery—are not uncommon to many women. I know now that no matter where we've come from, or what has passed in our lives, none of it matters. What matters is *what we choose to do now.* Today deals us a new hand, no matter which cards we were dealt before.

The gains in my life took hard effort, a willingness to leave the past behind, and a commitment to rejuvenate my soul with the goodness in the world.

When I realized I was the one who'd be solely responsible for myself and my daughter, my real business journey began. I convinced a dentist to train me to be a dental assistant in return for working for him for free and worked another full-time job to support us. The dentist secured a paying job for me with another dentist, but it would be two years before I had a full day off.

My knowledge of dental tools and how the products worked was rewarded when I was hired as the first female dental manufacturers' representative in the United States. I traveled across the country to work with other dental representatives (at that time all male), demonstrating our products on the dentists' patients, a sales technique not available to my male colleagues. I was not happy that the male sales reps made at least *six* times my salary, but my boss told me to be grateful for what I was earning because I was making top secretarial wages. Seriously? Equal pay for equal work was not even a glimmer in executives' eyes at that point.

Though I never reached wage parity, the owner of the business, George Seymour, became the first real mentor I ever had in my life. He taught me to travel on my own and made sure I was educated to succeed in a field that was considered men's business. I admit I was thrilled with the experience I gained and some of the perks of a salesperson's job—the travel, the chance adventure—even though I was still having to take extra part-time work to survive. My life had taken a corporate turn and I found it very different from the dysfunctional life I'd grown up in. I was eager, ambitious, and I knew I wanted to do something important with my life. I began learning about the world, other people, and myself.

When I joined Yellow Pages, my knowledge and my confidence grew exponentially as I learned marketing, advertising, public and community relations, and speaking, adding to my innate and learned sales skills. I was fortunate to have a manager early on that encouraged and supported my ideas and projects that were out of the norm for the longtime ways of doing business. That is when I began a lifetime commitment to self-improvement and personal development.

I started giving back to my community in many ways, including fundraising for charities and putting on community events. While sitting on a board for a home for battered and abused women and children, I did capital fundraising for a beautiful facility specially designed for children. When I became president of the Phoenix Ad Council, I became even more involved in causes and opened my world wider.

The telephone industry began its death spiral in the last few years of the twentieth century, and I left Yellow Pages to start a company with a partner. We went into cause-related marketing, publishing children's books that were sponsored by corporations, with a percentage of the profits going to children's hospitals. After we parted ways, I worked as a marketing consultant for small businesses, but found most clients didn't have the money to pay me; instead, they wanted to give me a percentage of ownership, which doesn't pay many bills. I'd been broke and underpaid before and wasn't about to regress.

With a new partner, I organized events and found immediate success; we were fearless and inventive, putting on huge rallies and events with marginal resources.

After a couple of years of booming business, I had the courage and resources—I thought—to launch an event of my own. I'd recently dedicated my life to Jesus Christ, and I felt called to create an event with a Christian focus. *Light in the Desert* was the name of my super-event, and I spent a year working with friends, family, and other believers to bring this dream to fruition. I rented the Peoria Sports Complex, which has a capacity of more than 12,000 people. I cashed in my 401k, stretched my cards to their max, and on April 24, 2000, the crowds finally came to share in my dream.

Just not enough of them.

My life crashed and burned again, and it took a while before I arose from the ashes this time. I was determined to repay every penny. I worked out a repayment plan with my creditors, liquidated my assets, and moved into a small, rented room at a friend's house.

229

This is the moment I reunited with cousin Bob and the next dramatic turn in my life took place. I rose from the ashes yet again.

I realized I'd made a mistake with my first rude judgment about network marketing. When I hear the occasional scornful comments about our industry, I think back to those days when I told Bob to "go get a job," and I laugh; people just don't know what they don't know. The truth is, network marketing has been a reliable and productive way to make money since the 1700s—long before retail stores even existed. While our industry has had its share of characters trying to turn a quick buck, they're in *every* industry, not just network marketing.

Once again, I was blessed to have a mentor. Bob

showed me the limitless possibilities available when we finally learn to step out of our comfort zones and believe in ourselves.

Network marketing is more than a career; it has given me extraordinary experiences, expanded my knowledge of the world, enriched my life with precious friends, and transformed both my self-worth and my net worth. These experiences and assets are not derivatives of products but rather sourced from the many kind, generous, and genuine people who held out their hands to help me up. That changed everything.

Because my passion is to coach and mentor women who, like me, have experienced abuse in their lives and are less than confident about who they are and what they can accomplish, I designed and launched *Women Building Bridges,* a program to teach women they are created for greatness and can accomplish their dreams. Four business partners and I traveled internationally to coach, mentor, and lift women, both personally and in business.

I tell them and tell you: Wherever you live on this planet, you, too, can rise from the ashes like a *phoenix* and transform *your* whole world. I have seen it. I have done it. I am living it.

If you are ready to move forward in your life, I offer my hand to help you up. Reach for it!

Dare to dream. Create a plan. Find a mentor. Then ***do*** *it.*

Author's Notes

When I was 14, and working at the local five-and-dime, I never could have predicted my current life as an international entrepreneur, speaker, executive coach, and author.

In my 20s, I became the first female manufacturer's rep of dental products in the country—at one-sixth of my male colleague's wages—and had to work two jobs to feed and care for my daughter. I spent years in the corporate arena at US West Direct, starting in sales and moving up to executive positions.

Finally, I decided it was past time to become my own boss, and I founded an event-planning business with a partner. A highlight was creating, developing, and running Arizona Bike week, which included 11 major events and 128 vendors over nine days with more than 200,000 motorcycle enthusiasts in attendance. It's still a Phoenix-area highlight.

I also owned Cause & Effect, LLC, which supplied employee evaluation and training, business plans, marketing strategies, and financial forecast development to startups and small companies.

Because I knew the needs of abused women and their families, I created fund-raising programs to help and shelter abused women.

Since joining the network marketing industry 18

years ago, I've built an organization of 175,000 people in 42 countries. I founded Women Building Bridges, an international organization that creates events for women to foster self-improvement and learn the fundamentals of owning their own business.

My community involvement includes serving on the boards of many organizations, including the Governor's Office for Children, Faith House, Family Christian Care, and the Hotel-Motel Association, plus serving as an arbitrator for the Better Business Bureau and as president of the Phoenix Advertising Club.

I am a member of the Multi-Million Dollar Club and recipient of the Phoenix 2018 Outstanding Leadership Award by the Global Women's Summit.

I co-authored *Mastering the Art of Success* with Les Brown and Jack Canfield, and *The Women's Millionaire Club* with Maureen G. Mulvaney.

Born in Southern California, I've been an Arizona resident most of my life. I cherish time spent with my family—daughter Cathy, and son Tommy; grandchildren: Preston, Christian, Gabriel, Nathaniel, Jerry, and Sierra; and great-grandchildren, Simon and Eliza.

Contact information

Email:	Carolyn@AnyOneCan.me
Website:	www.carolynmjohnson.com
Facebook:	carolyn.johnson.501
Instagram:	carolynpersonal
Linkedin:	carolyn-johnson-global-entrepreneur-1b437b16/
Twitter:	CarolynJohnson_

Chapter 20

Nothing Changes if Nothing Changes

Nic Kalo

If you said to me two years ago, "Nic, you'll co-author a Johnny Wimbrey book and share your life journey with the world," I would have said, "Get off the drugs!" and handed you a flyer for your local Narcotics Anonymous meeting.

Why? For 26 years, I was detached from reality because drug addiction ruled *my* life. I had a single goal every day: **Get high!** That was it. Every morning I would wake up with the same mission and do whatever I needed to score drugs.

Now, I wake up every morning with new goals:

Become one percent better than I was yesterday, continue to work every day to reach my goals and dreams, and maintain my mindset.

I can't blame childhood trauma and my family for my addiction. I had a great childhood with loving parents and a younger brother, and we were all close. My parents were good cop/bad cop. Mum was the one who handed out the punishments, and Dad let me get away with everything.

Dad and I were best friends. We lived together, worked together, played basketball together, and in our spare time, we went to the casino together. We could spend every waking minute together, and we never got sick of each other's company. Everyone loved my dad. Everyone knew who he was, that funny guy who would give you the shirt off his back. I idolized my dad. He was my hero.

Discomfort is where the magic of growth happens

234

The day Dad came home and told me he had cancer is burned into my memory. I was leaving the house to go and score my drugs when he pulled up from his doctor's appointment. We met on the lawn, and I could tell the news wasn't good.

Dad looked at me and said, "I have cancer, but I'll be okay." His face already looked defeated. We hugged, and I got into my car.

On the way to score my drugs, I drove the fastest I'd ever driven. My dad just told me he was about to fight his toughest battle and all I could think about was getting high and numbing my feelings. That's how my life was for 26 years. I chased that high so I didn't have to deal with life.

I began using drugs when I was 15, and I moved on to heroin when I was 19 and in an abusive relationship. My boyfriend threatened to kill me if I left him, and he locked all the doors to keep me from leaving. I was scared for my life, but I zoned out on heroin as a coping mechanism. It took me three years, but I finally worked up the courage to escape through a window.

I was hooked, and even after leaving the relationship, I continued using anything I could get my hands onto. I hit rock bottom more times than I can remember. Three times, my family gave me an ultimatum and forced me into rehab. I agreed to go, but I had no intention of really quitting. My longest clean stretch was about 20 days because I continued using the entire time I was in rehab. Each time I left, I walked out just as addicted, if not more so.

After my rehab attempts, I became so good at hiding my using that my partner didn't even know. I had two lives—the family woman and the junkie. As I continued using drugs, it got worse. I always had money for drugs, but I stole, begged, and lied to get it. I became a professional shoplifter, complete with a customer base. I took orders for specific products and ran my illicit business like a legitimate one.

As shops added more security and modern technology made the game harder, shoplifting began getting riskier. I didn't want to work for someone in an

235

ordinary job, so I looked for new ways to make money from home.

A friend mentioned cryptocurrency, and I had never heard of it before. He said, "Yeah you can trade it like stocks, and do it from your phone whenever you want."

That sounded like *my* type of gig. He texted the website of a trading academy where they teach you how to trade, and this is where my story really begins.

After I looked into it, I thought, *Why not give this thing a try? This shopping gig won't last much longer and I'm getting a little desperate.* I signed up.

I had no intention of quitting drugs. In fact, I was certain I would make a ton of money from trading because by that time I was using speed and I could stay up as late as I wanted. I figured I could be on the charts all day and night trading and become wealthy within six months. School had never interested me, and I'd dropped out when I was 16. So here I was, drugged up and trying to learn how to trade markets online.

Within the first month I got right into the study. I felt confident because of the drugs I was taking, even feeling somewhat cocky that I'd soon be rich. I kept hearing the experts say for someone to become a professional trader, they need to use 80% psychology and 20% technical analysis. Hmmmm . . . psychology, huh? That was nothing I wanted to investigate. I mean seriously, I didn't want to do any personal development or mindset work to become the best version of myself. I kept thinking, *I'm in great shape! My head is fine but thank you anyway!*

I didn't realize that the academy was also a

community of people with the same goals. Everyone was lifting and motivating each other to be the best versions of themselves and to help others on their journey. Despite myself, I couldn't avoid picking up snippets of personal development and mindset training during my team's live Zoom calls.

Though I wasn't trying, I was starting to learn about myself and what made me function best. I began to stay home a little more, locking myself away to study. Before long, I found myself enjoying being within a community of great people.

Five months into my trading journey, an out-of-state event was coming up. I didn't have any money at the time, but money was something I was great at making quickly. I really liked the idea of flying to the meeting to hang out and learn from the people whom I had only met on Zoom calls, but I knew if I flew with drugs, the strict airport security guaranteed I'd be caught with my stash.

My quandary was this: Do I stay at home so I can continue using drugs, or do I give this personal development and trading gig a shot and put the drugs down?

Lucky for me, I made the right decision. That weekend I gathered whatever saleable items I had in my house, and I sold them from a stall at a local market, legitimately earning enough money for my flight and accommodations. Then I went cold turkey and stopped taking drugs five days before my flight so I could get through the withdrawal symptoms. When I flew to the event, I was sober for the first time in decades.

At that first event, I realized that I've made a major change in how I think and act. My life has become focused on leveling up. Every time I reach a wall, I keep hitting it until it falls down and I can walk right through it. I can't tell you how many walls I have broken through in the last two years.

I'm not going to minimize how difficult it's been for me. Breaking down these walls to get to my next level has been the hardest thing I have ever had to do. But it does get easier each time.

I am honored to share what I've learned and what works for me.

Wisely choose the people you let into your circle. Mine includes some exceptionally powerful people. You can't be great and achieve amazing levels if your circle is not powerful. Proximity is power! That was a tough lesson for me because I loved pleasing people. I had thought giving people what they want would make them happy, which would make them like me, and we'd all win. How wrong I was! I have learned to be more selfish about who I let into my life. My mindset has changed. Love yourself first.

My circle is made up of people from every walk of life, and we all have the same goal: *To be the best we can be.*

Our shared mindset of *You got this, this will happen!* does truly make it happen. I could give you so many examples of when I feel I'm facing a tough situation and express my doubts to my circle. Suddenly, 10 members of my group are in my corner saying *You are not giving up on this. We will make this happen, just keep pushing.*

DO NOT GIVE UP NOW!

I can give you many more examples of my head trying to sabotage me because I'm in a too-comfortable place. My mind's telling me to stay cozy and safe right there—and then 10 members of my circle explain why I'm feeling that way and advise me about what I should do next. Every single time without fail I learn I'm just facing another wall, and I need to break that sucker down so I can walk through and fight my way to my next level.

Now I'm aware of these lessons whenever they're happening. I've learned if something doesn't feel right, I'm missing something. The solution is to voice what I'm feeling to my circle and get input into why I'm feeling that way. I guarantee, it's the most powerful feeling in the world when you've reached the point in your life when you can realize the next lesson and break down the next wall.

Each time you break down another wall and move to the new level, you become more powerful. Your confidence grows. You start believing what everyone is telling you, and you realize you *can* do this, you *have* found your purpose, you *are* on your way to becoming the best version of yourself.

The absolute best part is that you get comfortable being *un*comfortable, because you know the higher you reach the stronger you get.

At first, I was terrified. I was filled with doubt. I had no confidence. I was too scared to try anything new because I was too scared of failing. My mindset was weak. Think about it: For 26 years I used drugs to

239

escape my feelings of hopelessness. I was sure I wasn't good enough and I would never amount to anything. Everything in my life has been changing.

I learned the trick is to never give up and to believe in yourself. During those times you can't believe in yourself, I learned you must have people around you to lift you and fill you with belief until you can believe again.

Don't get me wrong, I still have days when I struggle, but they are less frequent. I no longer look at myself as a drug addict. I don't even say I am a recovering drug addict anymore. I *have* recovered.

I'm a new person with a million life lessons to share with the world. I wake up with a new mission, with a new purpose: *How can I help people who believe they're stuck in their lives? What can I do to inspire people to become the best versions of themselves?*

Why? Because I was there. I know how it feels to be stuck with no direction and no purpose in life. It's a horrible existence. It's not living. It's a dark and lonely place.

Yes, I have some motives for pushing myself so hard and changing my life. They are:

Myself. I finally respect and love myself enough to want more for *me*. I know I have an amazing story to tell. I know that my story could be someone's survival guide. I know why I am here. I love receiving messages from people saying that my story is inspiring them to grow and change their lives. There's no better feeling in the world.

My family. The journey of self-discovery has made

240

me realize how important it is to be more connected with my family. Our family life is the best it has ever been, open and honest, and the family unit is stronger. I have more time and money now, and I want to take my children on holidays to experience history and new cultures. I want them to experience life in the most amazing way.

My dad's cancer finally overcame him while I was still using drugs. He hadn't seen me clean since I was 19. When he was dying, I leaned over and whispered in his ear, "Dad, I will make you proud of me one day." I know he is up in heaven looking down on me, incredibly proud of the person I have become. Now I choose to keep my promise and make him proud every day.

Here are the key points I want to share with you:

Go through life with a purpose–to reach new levels of knowledge and achievement.

Choose the people in your circle carefully. Remember, not everyone will cheer for you, and that's okay, but keep the ones who don't support you at arms' length.

Call on your circle for support when you have those inevitable moments of doubt. They will help you get past your qualms when you feel you can not move.

Get comfortable with being uncomfortable. Discomfort is where the magic of growth happens. If your head is telling you not to leave your comfort zone, it's a good sign that you need to leave.

Always find the lesson. Be aware of what is happening to you and how you feel. Once you find the lesson, then you can continue and move forward to a new level.

Help others. Share what you've learned *and* the

mistakes you've made. Sharing also helps you by reinforcing your awareness that you do know what you're talking about. Sharing also reminds you of those key moments in your life—the struggles and challenges you went through. You'll remember how hard they were and exactly why you never want to regress to that early place in your growth.

You don't need to hit rock bottom before you want more for yourself. As I openly admit, I've hit rock bottom many times, way too many times to remember. Now I realize you don't need to be homeless and lose your friends and family before you decide *enough is enough!* You are in control of your life. You are where you are because of the decisions *you* have made.

Nothing changes if nothing changes.

242

Don't be afraid of failure. If you're scared, you will never try anything new. Of course, there will be times when you fail, but look at failure as a steppingstone to success. Learn from your mistakes. This knowledge will build your character and pave your way to your goal. Find out what drives you. Find out what you are passionate about. Then, put the blinkers on and run for your life!

Life is a journey. You will have hard moments and you will have amazing unforgettable moments. It's most helpful to become aware of how you react to the hard moments, because hard moments are when you build your mental wealth.

I can tell you firsthand, when you break through those hard moments and walk out the other end, you level up.

In less than two years, I've totally changed the direction of my life. I wake up every morning grateful for another day. I have come too far to stop now. Every day I work on my mindset, my mental wealth. I listen to personal development audios, read a book, or speak to my mentors. All these actions are incorporated into my daily routine.

My journey has only just begun. I have huge goals and I'll reach them because I believe in myself. I have an amazing circle of people around me, and an increasing number of people count on me. I take this responsibility seriously.

The only way I can lose now is if I quit. Quitting is not an option! **Never give up!**

Author's Notes

With hard work and much support from my circle of incredible mentors and friends, in less than two years I've evolved from someone who had been in active addiction for 26 years into a successful, independent investor who can inspire others to believe in themselves.

I discovered my skill as an effective mindset coach, and

I'm beginning to share this mental wealth with others. I will be going to schools and educating teenagers about peer group pressure, the importance of a good mindset, and how unimaginably destructive a life of drug addiction becomes.

I live in Melbourne, Australia, where I was born, with my three wonderful children, ages 7, 8, and 18.

My portion of this book is dedicated to my dad, who has been guiding me through this process. I promise him that the best is yet to come.

Contact Information

Email: nickalomba@gmail.com
Facebook: nic kalo
TikTok: @nic.kalo

Chapter 21

Grow Continuously

Les Brown

There's a saying that goes, *If the shoe fits, wear it.* But my mother, Mamie Brown, lived by a different saying: *If the shoe don't fit, make it fit!*

I remember Mama bringing home hand-me-down clothes at Christmastime from the families she worked for. One Christmas, she brought home some nice size eight leather shoes from one of the families. When I tried on the shoes, I couldn't get my feet into them because they weren't big enough.

When I told Mama I couldn't fit into them, I figured that would be the end of it. However, Mama called my sister, Margaret Ann, and told her to run some warm water into the bathtub and bring her some Vaseline. My sister did as she was told. As the water was running, Mama began rubbing my feet with Vaseline, then she stuffed my feet into those too-small shoes!

She instructed me to get into the tub and walk around in the water. "And you better not splash any water on the floor while you walking, either!"

I didn't know what the point was, so after walking around in the tub for a little while, I called Mama to let her know that the shoes still didn't fit. But she answered back, "Walk until they do!" I walked backward and forward for what seemed like forever. And, much to my surprise, after so many laps in the tub, the water-soaked leather became a comfortable eight-and-a-half—just my size!

It doesn't really matter what happens to you. What matters is how you deal with it!

If it had been up to me, I would have just given up on having those nice leather shoes, because they didn't fit me. I didn't know they could be *stretched* into a perfect fit.

This reminds me of how people treat their dreams and goals. Many people refuse to stretch themselves because they feel *they don't fit* the requirements or can't measure up to the demands of what it will take to get there. The truth of the matter is, if you don't try, you will never know what you can or cannot do.

No matter what you think you know, you don't know

enough about yourself to even doubt your own abilities. According to the laws of aerodynamics, a bumblebee isn't supposed to be able to fly because its puny little wings are not big enough to hold up its large body. It's a good thing for bumblebees that they never studied aerodynamics and don't know about their ill-designed bodies. Despite what science says, they continue to fly anyway!

Sometimes you need to be *intelligently ignorant.* When you're targeted to be the victim of policies, politics, religions, cultures, ad environments that are stacked against you—systems put into place and intentionally designed to destroy your sense of self—you must be like the bumblebee.

Just like my shoes, you must **grow continuously!** There will be times in our life when you feel that you can't overcome the odds. However, when you continue to work on yourself and develop mental resolve, increase your skills, and surround yourself with nourishing relationships, you will be able to defeat whatever obstacles life throws your way.

Walk those laps around the tub of life until the shoe fits! Don't allow your circumstances to define who you are; create the circumstances you want for yourself! Stretch yourself until you fit the occasion and meet the requirements.

Standing in a wheelchair

I've listened to hundreds of thousands of motivational messages to expand my mind, to raise my own bar, to challenge myself to reach beyond my comfort zone. Why? Because I know *to have something you've never had before, you have to become someone you've never been before.*

There is no way to know when all of the motivation that I've filled myself up with will be put to the test of application. But trust me, those tests *always* come!

One day, my son, Patrick, was pushing me through the airport in a wheelchair. It was the first time that I'd been in public without being able to walk. As you can probably imagine, I was embarrassed. I hung my head down, hoping that people would not recognize me, but many did and greeted me warmly. I tried to hide my feelings, but their facial expressions were clear; they felt sorry for me and some wanted to ask what happened.

In the middle of my embarrassment, I paused to ask myself, *Why are you ashamed that the people you're going to speak to will know your condition?*

248

I realized that I needed to grow and stretch myself for this new challenge and I certainly rose to the occasion. Even though I spoke on stage from a wheelchair, I received a standing ovation from the audience. It really encouraged me to know that people did not judge me because of my condition. They were focused on my message, and although I could not physically stand up, I stood up through all of them when I received their ovation! My *hunger* stood up in me and in them.

You must realize things are going to happen to you in life—things you can't even begin to imagine. It doesn't matter what happens to you. What matters is how you deal with it! I no longer need a wheelchair to get around, but even if I did, I would not hang my head down. I will always hold my head up high!

I should never have cared about the stares of the

people looking with their questioning expressions because I realize in that experience there was an opportunity for me to *grow continuously*. That is true for every experience, no matter how uncomfortable or humiliating.

Do not ever again let people—whether they're for you or against you—determine your level of growth and greatness! It's up to you to **grow continuously** *in every situation.*

Either you expand or you're expendable

To build my speaking business, I made so many calls that at one time I had a callous on my ear (people thought it was a big mole). I made over 100 calls each day. I even made calls on the weekends, when businesses were closed, just in case somebody was working overtime. Lo and behold, one day someone answered the phone on Sunday afternoon, and I met my first corporate client.

I had a dream of doing corporate training. As I methodically went through my list of contacts, I dialed the number for Michigan Bell corporate offices, a huge phone company. Someone picked up and I greeted him, saying, "Hello! My name is Les Brown. Do you, or someone you know, need a speaker to come in and motivate the salespeople to increase their performance?"

Bewildered, the person on the other end of the line said, "Do you know this is Sunday afternoon?"

I responded with just as much confidence as he'd projected bewilderment. "Yes, I do!" And I thought to myself, *Whoever's in working on the weekend is the*

249

person I need to talk to!

He told me to come in the next morning so we could speak face-to-face. And that's how I landed my first corporate contract! I trained employees from Michigan Bell, Illinois Bell, Sprint, and AT&T—all because I was willing to do the things that others won't do.

No matter what your passion is or your dream is, you will have to learn to master it. A recent book came out with the message, "Average is over!" The question is: One day, will you look back in regret or delight for how you handled your dreams?

Maybe it seems extreme, making 100 calls a day to the point of getting a calloused ear. And you know what? It *was* extreme. I missed out on time with friends and family. I missed out on rest. I missed out on recreation, but that's what it took for the reward that I enjoy today. I don't regret what I missed. I delight in what I've gained, and how I've impacted the lives of billions of people around the world.

Make no mistake about it. If you're not growing, you're shrinking! We live in an area that literally operates at lightning speed. If you aren't plugged in, you're left out. Now, more than ever, it's critical to constantly reach further and *grow continuously!*

Alvin Toffler, the author of *Future Shock,* made a profound statement: "The illiterate of the twenty-first century will not be those who cannot read and write, but those who cannot learn, unlearn and relearn." He was right. Change is constant, particularly in this era. Being flexible and willing to *grow continuously* are the new basic requirements for success.

Advances in technology allow businesses to move at the speed of light and the direction can change in a millisecond. As the great Robert Shuler said, "We're living in a time where you either expand or you are expendable." You must be nimble enough to ride the waves of change or you will crash and drown. Maybe if I were in that same position today, working to build my speaking business, I'd send out 100 texts a day or make 100 social media connections or set up 100 webinars!

You need to understand what it is going to take to win at what you're pursuing. You must continue to train and educate yourself to remain relevant. *You must grow continuously. You've got to be HUNGRY!*

Sharpening your ax

Abraham Lincoln said, "If I had six hours to chop a tree down, I'd spend four sharpening my ax." The strongest tool *you* have is your mind. We must constantly sharpen and develop our minds. I agree with American's foremost business philosopher and writer, Peter Drucker, who said, "This is an era of accelerated change, overwhelming complexity, and tremendous competition, facing us all."

A huge proportion of America's jobs will be permanently eliminated in the next few years due to the rise of artificial intelligence (AI), technology, cheap labor abroad, and apps. This doesn't even count job losses that have happened due to the pandemic. This is a time in which job security no longer exists. This is a time when you must have the mindset of an entrepreneur, control your own personal economy, create your own jobs, and make your own impact! *We're coming to the end of work!*

According to the Department of Labor, *before* the COVID-19 pandemic, more than 20,000 people were losing their jobs each month. During the pandemic, a million people were losing their jobs each *week.* Many others had pay cuts or hours cut. Too many of these jobs will never return.

The days of the 40/40/40 plan have come to an end. Working 40 hours a week for 40 years to receive 40 percent of your income is no longer a realistic plan, and not even an option after the employment market imploded in 2020. This is the time to ask yourself, *What is my strategy for being here? What's my next move?*

252 Sadly, so many people focus on making a living instead of living their making. Studies show Monday mornings have a thirty percent increase in heart attacks. People wake up to the grim reality of spending another forty-plus hours at a dreaded job they despise, and they often die on the toilet. So, you have a choice: To reduce your risk of a heart attack, you can either stop going to the toilet on Monday mornings, or you can start living the life you desire to live!

You must *grow continuously.* Grow in terms of your talents and skills and every area of your life. Put yourself in a position to get out of that dead-end job! As Mamie Brown always said, "Used-to-bees don't make no honey!" Never mind who or what you used to be. **Who and what are you now?** This is the time that you must challenge yourself! This is the time to develop at least three core competencies—three things that you are skilled enough to do to get paid for them. Become the person who can earn a living doing what you love!

Jim Rohn, who helped millions of people improve their lives, once said, "Work harder on yourself than on your job."

In the middle of the 2008 economic recession, Warren Buffet was asked what the most important investment was that people should make. This is a man who has made billions of dollars in the stock market and real estate. He answered, "The most important investment you can make is in yourself.

Mr. Buffett was correct—*you* are your greatest asset.

As an asset, you must find ways to appreciate it. Sometimes it's still hard for me to believe that I earn more in one hour than most Americans will earn in an entire year. I don't share this to impress you, but to impress upon you that:

We shouldn't work to get paid by the hour;
we should work to get paid
for the value we bring to the hour!

I want you to understand the power of investing in yourself. Knowledge is the new currency. Investing in yourself will yield the most profitable ROI (return on investment). Most of us never use the power that we have because we live in a world where we're told more about our limitations than our potential. This is why we must take the time to invest in our minds. We must acquire the knowledge to expand our vision of ourselves. We must "sharpen our ax," sharpen our thinking and sharpen our skills. We must *grow continuously.*

Don't ever let fear hold you hostage. Now, more than ever is the time to grow, learn, strengthen your mind and your skills, and choose your future.

Author's Notes

I grew up with two mothers, the one who gave my twin brother and me life, and the one who gave us love, Mamie Brown. We grew up in poverty in Liberty, City, Florida, and people told me to give up my dreams—they said I was the dumb twin. I knew, however, that my dreams were possible and I refused to give up. I had a hunger to take care of my mother, and I wanted to make a difference in the world.

255

I started in radio, filling in for a DJ when he became inebriated and couldn't do the show, and then getting a radio show of my own. I became a community activist, a state legislator for three terms in Ohio, and then moved into training and motivational speaking, something I wanted to do my entire life. For more than 50 years I've been teaching people how to overcome their obstacles, become one with their gifts, and share those gifts with the world.

Contact Information

Website: lesbrown.com
Facebook: The Les Brown
Instagram: @The Les Brown

Made in the USA
Middletown, DE
06 February 2023

23597717R00149